Introduction

With The Advent Of Technological Advancements In The Traditions And Cultures Of Marital Life In India, A New Problem Is Emerging – Fake Matrimonial Cases. This Has Become A Concern Especially For Indian Husbands, Who Often Become Victims Of Injustice And Baseless Allegations.

This Book Is An Attempt To Understand This Serious Problem And Take Steps Towards Its Solution. Here We Will Examine Various Aspects – Legal, Social, And Human Rights. We'll Learn The Stories Of Husbands Who Faced Their Own Challenges In This Incredible Struggle. And Won A Decisive Judicial Battle Which Became An Example.

In Indian Society, Marriage Is Seen As A Sacred Sacrament, Which Is The Basis Of Relationships And A Symbol Of Solitude. However, This Purity Is Currently Facing Many Indiscriminate Problems, One Of Which Is Fake Marriage Cases. This Book Communicates The Problems That Are Faced By Indian Husbands Who Are Victims Of Fraudulent Matrimonial Cases, Focuses On Their Effects, And Considers The Need For Society And The Legal System To Take Steps To Address This Problem. Is.

This Book Attempts To Bring About A Change In The Direction Of Husbands And Make Them Aware To Motivate Them For Positive Changes In Their Married Life. The Aim Of This Book Is To Create Awareness In The Society, So That It Can Change In A Positive Direction Towards Problem Solving.

In This Book, We Will Discuss About Fake Matrimonial Cases In Which Indian Husbands Face Injustice. We Will Examine Their Causes, Effects, And Various Approaches To Resolution. The Main Objective Of This Book Is To Increase The Understanding Of This Important Issue In The Indian Society And Create A Positive Change For Prosperous Marital Relationships.

Overall, Acknowledging And Addressing Fake Matrimonial Cases Issue Perpetrated By Wives Against Husbands Is Essential For Promoting Gender Equality, Safeguarding The Rights And Well-Being Of All Individuals, And Creating Safer, More Supportive Environments For Victims Of Fake Matrimonial Cases, Regardless Of Their Gender.

Here's An Overview Of The Main Laws And Regulations Governing Marriage In India:

1. Hindu Marriage Act, 1955:

•**Applicability**: The Hindu Marriage Act Applies To Hindus, Buddhists, Jains, And Sikhs. It Governs The Solemnization And Registration Of Marriages Among These Communities.

•**Conditions For Marriage**: The Act Specifies Conditions For A Valid Hindu Marriage, Including Age Of Marriage, Mental Capacity, Absence Of Prohibited Relationships, And Monogamy.

•**Ceremonial Requirements**: Hindu Marriages Are Typically Solemnized Through Traditional Rituals And Ceremonies, Followed By Registration Under The Act To Make The Marriage Legally Valid.

•**Grounds For Divorce**: The Act Provides Grounds For Divorce, Including Adultery, Cruelty, Desertion, Conversion To Another Religion, Mental Illness, And Incurable Diseases.

2   Special Marriage Act, 1954:

•Applicability: The Special Marriage Act Applies To All Citizens Of India Irrespective Of Religion Or Faith. It Allows Individuals To Marry Outside Their Own Religion Or Faith.

•Conditions For Marriage: Under This Act, Parties Intending To Marry Must Give Notice To The Marriage Officer, Who Publishes The Notice To Invite Objections. After The Specified Waiting Period, The Marriage Can Be Solemnized.

•Marriage Procedure: The Act Provides For A Secular Marriage Ceremony Conducted Before A Marriage Officer, Followed By Registration Of The Marriage.

•Grounds For Divorce: The Grounds For Divorce Under The Special Marriage Act Are Similar To Those Under The Hindu Marriage Act, Including Adultery, Cruelty, Desertion, And Conversion.

3   Muslim Personal Law:

•Applicability: Matrimonial Matters Among Muslims Are Governed By Islamic Personal Law, Which Includes The Shariah And Principles Derived From Quranic Injunctions And Hadiths.

•Conditions For Marriage: Under Muslim Law, Marriage Is A Civil Contract Between Parties. Essential Elements Include Offer (Ijab) By One Party And Acceptance (Qabul) By The Other In The Presence Of Witnesses.

•Ceremonial Requirements: Muslim Marriages Are Solemnized Through The Nikah Ceremony, Which Involves The Recitation Of Marriage Vows By The Bride And Groom In The Presence Of Witnesses And A Qazi Or Maulvi.

•Dissolution Of Marriage: Muslim Law Provides For Various Forms Of Divorce, Including Talaq (Divorce By Husband), Khula (Divorce By Mutual Consent), And Judicial Divorce.

4   *Christian Marriage Law:*

•**Applicability:** Matrimonial Matters Among Christians Are Governed By The Indian Christian Marriage Act, 1872, And The Divorce Act, 1869.

•**Conditions For Marriage:** Christian Marriages Must Be Solemnized By A Licensed Minister Or Priest And Registered Under The Act To Be Legally Valid.

•**Ceremonial Requirements:** Christian Marriages Typically Involve A Religious Ceremony Conducted In A Church, Followed By Registration Of The Marriage.

•**Grounds For Divorce:** The Divorce Act Provides Grounds For Divorce, Including Adultery, Cruelty, Desertion, And Conversion.

5.   *Parsi Marriage And Divorce Law:*

•**Applicability:** The Parsi Marriage And Divorce Act, 1936, Governs Matrimonial Matters Among Parsis (Zoroastrians) In India.

•**Conditions For Marriage:** Parsi Marriages Must Be Solemnized As Per Parsi Customs And Registered Under The Act.

•**Ceremonial Requirements:** Parsi Marriages Involve Ceremonies Conducted In The Presence Of A Parsi Priest And Witnesses.

•**Grounds For Divorce:** The Act Provides Grounds For Divorce, Including Adultery, Cruelty, Desertion, And Conversion.

These Are Some Of The Main Laws And Regulations Governing Marriage In India, Catering To Different Religious Communities And Providing Legal Frameworks For Solemnization, Registration, And Dissolution Of Marriages

In India, Matrimonial Law Encompasses Various Statutes & Legal Provisions That Govern Marriage, Divorce, Alimony, Child Custody, And Related Matters. While These Laws Are Intended To Protect The Rights And Interests Of Both Spouses, There Have Been Concerns About Misuse And Abuse Of Legal Provisions Against Husbands. Some Common Legal Frameworks And Provisions That Indian Husbands May Encounter In Matrimonial Disputes Include:

Domestic Violence Act (DVA) 2005:

The DVA Provides Protection To Victims Of Domestic Violence, Including Wives. However, There Have Been Instances Where Husbands Have Been Falsely Accused Under This Law. The Act Defines Various Forms Of Domestic Violence, Including Physical, Emotional, Sexual, And Economic Abuse.

Dowry Prohibition Act 1961:

This Law Prohibits The Giving Or Receiving Of Dowry In Connection With Marriage. Despite Its Intention To Prevent Dowry-Related Harassment, Husbands And Their Families Have Sometimes Been Falsely Accused Under This Act.

Section 498A Of The Indian Penal Code (IPC):

This Provision Deals With Cruelty By Husbands Or Relatives Of Husbands Towards A Married Woman. While It Aims To Protect Women From Harassment And Cruelty, There Have Been Cases Of Misuse Where Husbands And Their Families Have Been Falsely Implicated.

Hindu Marriage Act 1955:

This Legislation Governs Marriage And Divorce Among Hindus In India. It Includes Provisions Related To Grounds For Divorce, Alimony, Child Custody, And Maintenance. Husbands May Face Legal Challenges Under This Act In Divorce Proceedings, Particularly Regarding Issues Such As Alimony And Property Division.

Guardians And Wards Act 1890:

In Cases Involving Child Custody Disputes, This Act Provides For The Appointment Of Guardians And Determines The Welfare Of The Child As The Paramount Consideration. Husbands May Seek Custody Of Their Children Under This Law, But They May Face Obstacles Due To Prevailing Societal Norms And Biases.

Maintenance & Welfare Of Parents & Senior Citizens Act 2007:

This Act Allows Parents, Including Fathers, To Claim Maintenance From Their Children If They Are Unable To Support Themselves. While This Law Primarily Focuses On The Welfare Of Parents, Husbands May Face Legal Obligations To Provide Maintenance To Their Parents, Adding Financial Strain In Some Cases.

Indian Divorce Laws:

Divorce Laws In India, Including The Hindu Marriage Act, The Special Marriage Act, And The Muslim Personal Law, Provide Grounds For Divorce And Procedures For Obtaining A Divorce. Husbands May Initiate Divorce Proceedings Or Respond To Divorce Petitions Filed By Their Wives, Leading To Legal Battles Over Issues Such As Grounds For Divorce, Alimony, And Child Custody.

It's Important To Note That While These Laws Are Intended To Protect Vulnerable Individuals And Promote Justice In Matrimonial Disputes, There Have Been Instances Of Misuse And Abuse, Leading To Hardships For Innocent Husbands And Their Families. Efforts To Reform And Strengthen The Legal Framework, Along With Awareness Campaigns And Legal Aid Services, Are Essential To Ensure Fairness And Prevent Injustice In Matrimonial Cases Involving Indian Husbands.

- False Allegations Of Domestic Violence:

Husbands Are Sometimes Falsely Accused Of Domestic Violence, Which Can Lead To Legal Battles And Social Stigma

- Dowry Harassment Claims:

There Have Been Instances Where Husbands And Their Families Are Wrongfully Accused Of Demanding Dowry, Leading To Legal Proceedings Under The Dowry Prohibition Act

- Misuse Of Section 498A:

Section 498A Of The Indian Penal Code, Which Deals With Cruelty By Husband Or Relatives, Is Sometimes Misused To File False Cases Against Husbands And Their Families

- False Charges Of Bigamy:

Men Have Been Falsely Accused Of Having More Than One Wife At The Same Time, Which Is A Criminal Offense In India

- Fake Profiles On Matrimonial Sites

There Have Been Reports Of Fake Profiles On Matrimonial Sites That Dupe Individuals, Including Trapping Men Into Fraudulent Relationships

The Supreme Court Of India Has Acknowledged The Misuse Of Laws Meant To Protect Women From Marital Abuse And Has Issued Guidelines To Prevent Such Misuse. For Instance, The Court Has Warned Against The Filing Of False Cases, Emphasizing The Need To Take A Serious View Of Such Incidents To Ensure That The Social Fabric Is Not Ruined

It's Important To Note That While There Are Genuine Cases Of Abuse And Harassment, The Misuse Of Laws Can Have A Detrimental Effect On The Lives Of Those Who Are Falsely Accused. The Legal System Continues To Evolve To Strike A Balance Between Protecting The Rights Of Women And Preventing The Misuse Of Laws. If You're Looking For More Detailed Information On Specific Cases Or Legal Advice, It Would Be Best To Consult A Legal Professional

False Allegations Of Domestic Violence

In A High-Profile Case, A Husband Was Falsely Accused Of Domestic Violence By His Wife Seeking To Gain Leverage In Their Divorce Proceedings. Despite Evidence Proving His Innocence, The Husband Faced Significant Legal And Social Challenges Until The Truth Emerged, And The False Allegations Were Debunked.

Fabricated Claims Of Dowry Harassment

A Husband And His Family Were Falsely Accused Of Dowry Harassment By The Wife's Family. Investigations Revealed That The Allegations Were Fabricated To Extort Money And Property From The Husband's Family. Legal Intervention Helped Expose The Truth And Exonerate The Innocent Parties.

Fraudulent Claims Of Infidelity:

In Another Case, A Wife Filed For Divorce, Citing Her Husband's Alleged Infidelity. However, Further Investigation Revealed That The Wife Had Fabricated Evidence And Coerced Witnesses To Support

Her False Claims. The Husband's Reputation Suffered Until He Could Prove His Innocence And The Deceitful Nature Of The Accusations.

Manipulative Child Custody Claims:

A Husband Faced A Contentious Child Custody Battle When His Wife Falsely Accused Him Of Being An Unfit Parent. Despite Being Actively Involved In His Children's Lives, The Husband Had To Navigate A Legal Minefield To Counter The Baseless Accusations And Secure Custody Rights.

Financial Deception And False Asset Claims:

In A Complex Divorce Case, A Husband Was Falsely Accused Of Hiding Assets To Avoid Equitable Distribution. Through Forensic Accounting And Legal Scrutiny, It Was Revealed That The Wife Had Exaggerated Her Claims And Attempted To Defraud Her Husband. The Truth Emerged During The Legal Proceedings, Safeguarding The Husband's Financial Interests.

These Examples Highlight The Challenges And Injustices Faced By Husbands In Fake Matrimonial Cases, Emphasizing The Importance Of Fair Legal Proceedings And Evidence-Based Decision-Making In Resolving Such Disputes

Impact Of Fake Matrimonial Cases On Husbands

The Impact Of Fake Matrimonial Cases On Husbands Can Be Profound And Far-Reaching, Affecting Various Aspects Of Their Lives Including:

Emotional Distress: Being Falsely Accused In A Matrimonial Dispute Can Result In Significant Emotional Distress For Husbands. They May Experience Feelings Of Anger, Frustration, Anxiety, And Betrayal, Particularly If The Accusations Come From Someone They Once Trusted.

Social Stigma: False Accusations Can Tarnish A Husband's Reputation Within His Family, Community, And Workplace. The Stigma Associated With Being Labelled As An Abuser Or Perpetrator Of Domestic Violence Can Lead To Social Isolation, Ostracism, And Damage To Personal And Professional Relationships.

Financial Burden: Defending Against False Accusations In Matrimonial Cases Can Impose A Substantial Financial Burden On Husbands. Legal Fees, Court Costs, And Other Related Expenses Can Drain Their Financial Resources And Jeopardize Their Economic Stability.

Legal Battles: Engaging In Protracted Legal Battles To Prove Their Innocence Can Be Emotionally And Financially Draining For Husbands. The Complexities Of The Legal System And The Adversarial Nature Of Litigation Can Exacerbate Stress And Anxiety, Prolonging The Resolution Of The Dispute.

Parental Alienation: False Accusations In Child Custody Disputes Can Lead To Parental Alienation, Where Husbands Are Unfairly Deprived Of Meaningful Relationships With Their Children. This Can Have Long-Term Consequences For Both The Husband And The Children, Affecting Their Emotional Well-Being And Family Dynamics.

Impact On Mental Health: The Cumulative Effect Of Facing False Accusations, Navigating Legal Proceedings, And Coping With The Associated Stressors Can Take A Toll On Husbands' Mental Health. They May Experience Depression, Anxiety Disorders, Post-Traumatic Stress Disorder (PTSD), And Other Psychological Issues As A Result Of The Ordeal.

Loss Of Trust: False Accusations Can Erode Trust And Confidence In Marital Relationships, Leading To Breakdowns In Communication And Intimacy. Even If The Accusations Are Ultimately Proven False, The Damage To Trust And The Sense Of Betrayal May Linger, Making It Difficult To Rebuild The Relationship.

Overall, The Impact Of Fake Matrimonial Cases On Husbands Extends Beyond The Legal Realm, Affecting Their Emotional Well-Being, Social Standing, Financial Stability, And Familial Relationships. It Underscores The Importance Of Addressing The Root Causes Of False Accusations And Ensuring Fair And Equitable Treatment For All Parties Involved In Matrimonial Disputes.

Solutions For The Challenges Posed By Fake Matrimonial Cases Against Husbands

Addressing The Challenges Posed By Fake Matrimonial Cases Against Husbands Requires A Multi-Faceted Approach Involving Legal, Social, And Educational Interventions. Here Are Some Potential Solutions:

Legal Reforms: Implementing Legal Reforms To Prevent Misuse Of Laws Intended To Protect Spouses From Domestic Violence And Harassment. This May Include Stricter Penalties For False Accusations And Provisions For Speedy Resolution Of Such Cases To Minimize The Impact On The Accused.

Legal Aid And Support: Providing Legal Aid And Support Services To Husbands Who Are Falsely Accused In Matrimonial Disputes. This Could Involve Establishing Dedicated Helplines, Legal Clinics, And Support Groups To Assist Husbands In Navigating The Legal System And Defending Their Rights.

Awareness Campaigns: Launching Public Awareness Campaigns To Educate Society About The Prevalence And Consequences Of False Matrimonial Cases. These Campaigns Can Help Dispel Myths And Stereotypes Surrounding Gender-Based Violence And Raise Awareness About The Need For Fair And Evidence-Based Legal Proceedings.

Mediation And Counselling: Encouraging Alternative Dispute Resolution Mechanisms Such As Mediation And Counselling To Resolve Matrimonial Disputes Amicably. Mediation Can Help Couples Negotiate Mutually Acceptable Solutions While Avoiding The Adversarial Nature Of Traditional Litigation.

Strengthening Judicial Oversight: Ensuring Robust Judicial Oversight To Prevent Miscarriages Of Justice In Matrimonial Cases. This May Involve Training Judges And Legal Professionals To Recognize Signs Of False Accusations And Apply Critical Scrutiny To Evidence Presented In Court.

Promoting Gender Equality: Promoting Gender Equality And Mutual Respect Within Marriages Through Educational Initiatives And Community Outreach Programs. By Challenging Traditional Gender Roles And Stereotypes, Society Can Foster Healthier Relationships Based On Mutual Trust And Understanding.

Support For Victims Of False Accusations: Providing Support And Rehabilitation Services To Husbands Who Have Been Falsely Accused In Matrimonial Cases. This May Include Counselling, Financial Assistance, And Measures To Rebuild Their Reputation And Livelihoods.

By Implementing These Solutions In A Coordinated Manner, Society Can Work Towards Addressing The Root Causes Of Fake Matrimonial Cases Against Husbands And Promoting Fairness, Justice, And Equality Within Marital Relationships.

Legal Remedies In Matrimonial Disputes

In Matrimonial Disputes, Husbands Have Several Legal Remedies Available To Them. Let's Explore Some Of These Options:

1. Restitution Of Conjugal Rights (Section 9):

• If Either The Wife Or The Husband, Without Reasonable Excuse, Decides To Withdraw From The Society Of Their Spouse, They Can Apply For Restitution Of Conjugal Rights. The Court May Pass A Decree For The Restitution Of Conjugal Rights If There Is No Legal Ground To Deny It

2. Judicial Separation (Section 10):

• Judicial Separation Implies Legal Separation Without Divorce. It Allows Spouses To Live Apart While Still Being Legally Married. Unlike Divorce, It Does Not Terminate The Marriage But Provides Relief From Cohabitation

3. Void And Voidable Marriages (Sec. 11 & 12):

• If A Marriage Is Void (Such As Due To Bigamy Or Lack Of Consent), It Is Considered Invalid From The Beginning. If It Is Voidable (Due To Factors Like Fraud Or Impotence), It Can Be Annulled By The Court

4. Divorce (Section 13):

- Divorce Is The Legal Cessation Of A Matrimonial Bond. Grounds For Divorce Include Cruelty, Adultery, Desertion, Conversion, Mental Illness, And More. The Court May Grant A Divorce If The Conditions Are Met.

5. Divorce By Mutual Consent (Section 13B):

- If Both Spouses Agree To Divorce, They Can File A Joint Petition For Divorce By Mutual Consent. After A Mandatory Waiting Period, The Court May Grant The Divorce.

Remember That Each Case Is Unique, And Legal Advice Should Be Sought Based On Specific Circumstances. Consulting A Legal Professional Is Crucial To Understanding The Best Course Of Action In Matrimonial Disputes.

How To Protect Your Assets During A Matrimonial Dispute

Protecting Your Assets During A Matrimonial Dispute Is A Critical Concern, And There Are Several Steps You Can Take To Safeguard Your Interests:

1. Documentation: Ensure All Property Ownership Documents Are Up-To-Date And Clearly State Your Ownership Rights.

2. Pre-Nuptial Agreements: If You're Not Yet Married, Consider A Pre-Nuptial Agreement That Outlines The Distribution Of Assets In The Event Of A Divorce.

3. Legal Consultation: Seek Advice From A Family Law Attorney Who Can Provide Guidance Specific To Your Situation And Jurisdiction

4. Financial Agreements: Create Financial Agreements That Are Legally Binding And Clarify The Terms Of Asset Division.

5. Estate Planning: Engage In Estate Planning, Including Creating Wills And Trusts, To Ensure Your Assets Are Managed According To Your Wishes.

6. Joint Ownership: If Possible, Convert Individual Ownership Into Joint Ownership With Someone You Trust, Which Can Sometimes Protect Assets From Being Claimed In A Dispute.

7. Trusts: Utilize Trusts To Legally Protect Your Assets. Assets Placed In A Trust May Be Shielded From Matrimonial Disputes.

Guardians Of Justice: The Judicial Response To Matrimonial Disputes And False Accusations Against Husbands

In Recent Years, Matrimonial Disputes In India Have Witnessed A Concerning Trend Of False Accusations And Misuse Of Legal Provisions, Particularly Against Husbands. These Cases, Often Fraught With Allegations Of Domestic Violence, Dowry Harassment, And Cruelty, Have Placed Undue Burdens On Innocent Individuals And Their Families, Causing Immense Emotional, Financial, And Social Distress.

Amidst These Challenges, The Judiciary, Represented By The Supreme Court And Various High Courts Across The Country, Has Played A Crucial Role In Upholding The Principles Of Justice, Fairness, And Equity. Through Landmark Judgments And Precedent-Setting Rulings, The Judiciary Has Provided Guidance, Clarity, And Safeguards To Protect The Rights Of Individuals Embroiled In Matrimonial Disputes, Particularly Husbands Facing False Accusations.

This Guide Aims To Provide A Comprehensive Resource For Husbands Seeking Solutions And Assistance Based On Supreme Court Judgments And High Court Rulings. Drawing Upon Legal Precedents And Case Law, This Guide Offers Practical Strategies, Legal Insights, And Support Services Tailored To Address The Unique Challenges Faced By Husbands In Matrimonial Disputes.

From Navigating The Complexities Of Legal Proceedings To Accessing Support Services And Seeking Redress For False Accusations, This Guide Serves As A Beacon Of Hope And Empowerment For Husbands Seeking Justice And Fairness In Their Marital Relationships. By Harnessing The Wisdom And Guidance Offered By The Judiciary, Husbands Can Assert Their Rights, Defend Their Dignity, And Reclaim Their Lives Amidst The Turmoil Of Matrimonial Disputes.

Through Collaboration, Advocacy, And Awareness, We Strive To Create A Society Where Matrimonial Justice Is Not Just A Legal Obligation But A Fundamental Cornerstone Of Fairness, Equality, And Human Dignity For All Individuals Involved. Together, Let Us Embark On This Journey Towards A Brighter Future, Where Justice Prevails, And Families Thrive In Harmony And Peace.

Unveiling Falsehoods:

Addressing Fabricated Cases Against Husbands & Defences

In Detail

Section 498A Of The Indian Penal Code (IPC)

Section 498A Deals With The Violence Perpetrated Against Women After Marriage By Their Husbands, In-Laws, Or Any Relative Of The Husband. Here Are The Key Points:

Note : In The Bhartiya Nyaya Sanhita, Dowry Cruelty Has Been Defined Under Section 85

1. Offense And Punishment:

> Whoever, Being The Husband Or A Relative Of The Husband Of A Woman, Subjects Such Woman To Cruelty Shall Be Punished With Imprisonment For A Term Which May Extend To Three Years And Shall Also Be Liable To A Fine.

> The Offense Committed Under Section 498A Is Cognizable, Non-Compoundable, And Non-Bailable.

2. Definition Of Cruelty:

> "Cruelty" Under This Section Can Be:

> Any Wilful Conduct Likely To Drive The Woman To Commit Suicide Or Cause Grave Injury Or Danger To Life, Limb, Or Health (Whether Mental Or Physical).

> Harassment Of The Woman With A View To Coercing Her Or Any Person Related To Her To Meet Any Unlawful Demand For Property Or Valuable Security, Or Due To Her Failure To Meet Such Demand.

3. Need For Section 498A:

> Women Have Historically Faced Cruelty Within Male-Dominated Societies.
> Laws Like Section 498A Empower Women To Fight Back And Seek Justice.
> In India, Where Dowry-Related Harassment Is Prevalent, Such Laws Play A Crucial Role In Preventing Cruelty Against Women.
> Despite Potential Misuse, These Laws Remain Essential For Protecting Married Women From Domestic Violence.

Remember That While Section 498A Serves An Important Purpose, It's Essential To Ensure Fair Implementation And Prevent Misuse.

Provision For Counselling Or Reconciliation Before Filing An FIR Under This Section

The Settlement (Reconciliation) Process Related To Section 498A Of The Indian Penal Code (IPC).

1. Mediation And Mutual Settlement

> While There Is No Specific "Settlement Process" Outlined In Section 498A, Cases Between A Husband And Wife Can Typically Be Resolved Through Mutual Settlement Or Compromise.

- Mediation Can Be Ordered By The Court As Part Of The Pre-Trial Process Or Initiated Voluntarily By The Parties.
- During Mediation, A Neutral Third Party (A Mediator) Helps The Parties Reach A Mutually Acceptable Solution.
- The Husband And His Family May Agree To Certain Terms (Such As Not Engaging In Further Acts Of Cruelty), And In Exchange, The Woman May Withdraw Her Complaint.

2. Application To Quash FIR:

- After Reaching A Compromise In A 498A Case, The Parties Can File An Application Under Section 482 Of The Code Of Criminal Procedure (Crpc) In The High Court.
- This Application Seeks To Quash (Dismiss) The First Information Report (FIR).
- The High Court Has The Power To Quash Criminal Proceedings If It Finds That The Proceeding Or FIR Is An Abuse Of The Court's Process Or Is Being Used To Oppress The Accused.

3. Court Approval:

- The Court Examines The Settlement And Decides Whether To Approve It.
- The Court Usually Approves A Mutual Settlement If It Is Fair, Just, And Serves The Ends Of Justice.
- Once Approved, The Court Orders The Withdrawal Of The Case, And Both Parties Must Withdraw Their Respective Complaints.

Remember That Even If A Mutual Settlement Is Reached, Court Approval Is Necessary. The Court Ensures That Justice Is Served While Protecting The Rights Of Both Parties.

Common Mistakes People Make When Defending Against False Accusations Under This Section

When Defending Against False Accusations Under Section 498A Of The Indian Penal Code (IPC), People May Inadvertently Make Certain Mistakes. Here Are Some Common Pitfalls To Avoid:

1. Overreacting Or Retaliating:

- When Faced With False Allegations, Emotions Can Run High. However, It's Essential To Remain Calm And Avoid Any Aggressive Or Retaliatory Behaviour.
- Overreacting Can Harm Your Case And May Be Used Against You.

2. Lack Of Proper Documentation:

- Failing To Maintain Records Of Conversations, Messages, Or Interactions Can Weaken Your Defence.
- Proper Documentation Can Help Prove Your Innocence And Disprove The Allegations.

3. Not Seeking Legal Counsel Early:

- Waiting Too Long To Consult A Lawyer Can Be Detrimental.
- Legal Advice Is Crucial From The Outset To Understand Your Rights, Build A Defence Strategy, And Navigate The Legal Process.

4. Ignoring Mediation Or Settlement Options:

- Mediation Can Be A Useful Tool To Resolve Disputes Amicably.
- Ignoring Mediation Or Settlement Opportunities May Prolong The Legal Battle Unnecessarily.

5. Not Leveraging Supreme Court Judgments:

- ➤ Recent Supreme Court Judgments Have Addressed Misuse Of Section 498A.
- ➤ Familiarize Yourself With These Judgments And Use Them To Strengthen Your Defence.

6. Failing To Challenge Specific Allegations:

- ➤ If The Allegations Lack Specificity Or Are Vague, Challenge Them In Court.
- ➤ Specificity Is Crucial For A Valid Case Under Section 498A.

7. Not Seeking Anticipatory Bail:

- ➤ If There's A Risk Of Arrest, Apply For Anticipatory Bail Promptly.
- ➤ It Prevents Unnecessary Custody And Allows You To Prepare Your Defence.

Defences Used In 498A Cases

In Order To Defend Oneself From Any Allegation Made Under IPC Sec. 498A There Are Several Steps A Husband Can Take:

1. Anticipatory Bail

- If The Husband Has Apprehensions That His Wife May File An FIR Under Section 498A, He Should Seek Anticipatory Bail.
- Anticipatory Bail Acts As A Precautionary Measure To Prevent The Husband's And His Family Members' Arrest.
- It Allows The Accused To Avoid Arrest If The Police Move Ahead With Any Such Action.

2. Strong Evidence:

- To Protect Himself, The Husband Must Gather Strong Documents And Evidence.
- Maintain Records Of Any Relevant Conversations, Phone Calls, Or Interactions.
- Witnesses Who Can Testify In Favor Of The Husband's Innocence Can Also Provide Crucial Evidence.

3. Legal Support

- Consulting A Knowledgeable Lawyer Is Essential.
- A Lawyer Can Guide The Husband On The Legal Aspects, Help Build A Strong Defence, And Ensure Proper Representation In Court.

Some More Common Defences That An Accused Person Can Consider:

1. Defamation:

- The Husband Has The Opportunity To File A Case Of Defamation Under Section 500 Of The Indian Penal Code, 1860.
- Defamation Can Be A Ground For Defence If A Case Has Been Filed By The Woman Or Wife Under Section 498A.
- Section 500 States That Whoever Defames Another Person Shall Be Punished With Simple Imprisonment For A Period Not Less Than Two Years Or With A Fine Or Both.

2. Civil Remedies:

- Under Section 9 Of The Civil Procedure Code, 1908, The Accused Person (Husband Or Relative) Can File An Application For The Recovery Of Damages.
- If The Accused And Their Family Have Suffered Due To False Accusations Of Cruelty And Harassment, This Provision Allows Them To Seek Compensation.
- While This May Not Directly Defend Against The Criminal Charges, It Helps In Recovering Damages Caused By Defamation.

3. Evidence Collection:

- Gathering Strong Evidence That Disproves The Allegations Made By The Complainant Is Crucial.
- Maintain Records Of Conversations, Interactions, And Any Relevant Documents.

> Witnesses Who Can Testify In Favor Of The Accused's Innocence Can Provide Valuable Evidence.

4. Supreme Court Guidelines:

> The Supreme Court Has Recognized The Misuse Of Section 498A.

> In The Arnesh Kumar V. State Of Bihar Case, The Court Laid Down Guidelines For Police Officers And Magistrates To Prevent Arbitrary Arrests.

> Arrests Under Section 498A Must Be Based On Reasonable Satisfaction Regarding The Genuineness Of The Allegation.

Using Supreme Court Judgments As A Defence Against False Allegations Under Section 498A

To Use Recent Supreme Court Judgments In Defence Against False Allegations Under Section 498A, One Can Follow These Steps:

1. Highlight Specificity In Allegations:

> Use The Judgment From Kahkashan Kausar V. State Of Bihar To Emphasize The Need For Specific Allegations Against The Husband's Relatives.

> If The Accusations Are Vague And Do Not Specify The Exact Role Or Action Of The Accused, This Judgment Can Be Used To Argue Against The Validity Of The Charges.

2. Seriousness Of Allegations By Female Relatives:

> Refer To The Judgment In Meera V. State, Which States That When An Offense Has Been Committed By A Woman Against Another Woman, It Becomes A More Serious Offense.

> This Can Be Used To Argue That Not All Allegations Are Equal And That Each Should Be Judged On Its Own Merits, Especially When They Come From Within The Family.

3. Prevent Arbitrary Arrests:

> Cite The Guidelines Laid Down In The Arnesh Kumar V. State Of Bihar Case, Which Were Set To Prevent Arbitrary Arrests Under Section 498A.

> These Guidelines Can Be Used To Argue Against Immediate Arrest Without Proper Investigation And Reasonable Satisfaction Of The Allegations' Genuineness.

> Consult With A Lawyer Who Is Well-Versed In These Judgments And Can Effectively Use Them In Court To Defend Against The Allegations.

> A Knowledgeable Lawyer Can Also Help Navigate The Legal System And Ensure That The Accused's Rights Are Protected.

>

It's Important To Remember That While These Judgments Can Be Helpful, Each Case Is Unique And Must Be Approached Based On Its Individual Facts And Circumstances.

To Challenge The Validity Of Specific Allegations Made Under Section 498A Of The IPC, An Accused Person Can Take The Following Steps:

1. Challenge The Allegations In Court:

- The Accused Can Challenge The Allegations Directly In Court.

- The Defence Can Argue That The Allegations Are Vague, Lack Specificity, Or Are Not Backed By Sufficient Evidence.

2. Use Supreme Court Judgments:

- Refer To Recent Supreme Court Judgments That Have Addressed The Issue Of Specificity In Allegations.

- These Judgments Can Be Used To Argue That Without Specific Allegations, The Case Should Not Proceed.

3. Quash The FIR:

- If The Allegations Are Found To Be Baseless Or Intentionally Vague, The Accused Can Approach The High Court To Quash The FIR Under Section 482 Of The Crpc.

It's Important To Approach Such Cases With A Clear Strategy And To Ensure That All Actions Taken Are Within The Bounds Of The Law.

Some Examples Of Cases Where Defence Strategies Against False Accusations Under Section 498A IPC Were Successful:

1. Geeta Mehrotra & Anr. V. State Of U.P. & Anr. (2012):

- In This Case, The Allahabad High Court Quashed The FIR Filed Under Section 498A IPC Against The Husband And His Family Members. The Court Recognized That The Allegations Were Baseless And Did Not Warrant Prosecution.

2. Preeti Gupta & Anr. V. State Of Jharkhand & Anr. (2010):

- The Supreme Court Observed That There Was A Tendency To Involve All Family Members In Matrimonial Disputes. The Court Quashed The Criminal Proceedings Against The Husband's Relatives, Noting That The Allegations Did Not Fit Within The Ambit Of Section 498A.

3. Sushil Kumar Sharma V. Union Of India (2005):

- The Supreme Court Criticized The Misuse Of Section 498A And Emphasized The Need For The Legislature To Find Ways To Prevent Such Misuse. This Case Highlighted The Importance Of Safeguarding The Rights Of The Accused Against Frivolous Complaints.

False Dowry Case

The Dowry Prohibition Act, 1961 Specifically Prohibits Giving Or Receiving Dowry. According To This Act, Dowry Means Any Property Or Valuable Security Given Or Agreed To Be Given Either Directly Or Indirectly By One Party In Marriage To The Other Party, Or By The Parents Of Either Party To A Marriage Or By Any Other

Person To Either Party As Consideration For The Marriage. However, It Does Not Include Dower Or Mahr In The Case Of Persons To Whom The Muslim Personal Law Applies.

Under The Dowry Prohibition Act, Any Act To Take Or Give Dowry Is Punishable In India. The Punishment For Violating The Anti-Dowry Law Includes Imprisonment For Up To 5 Years And A Fine Of Rs. 15,000 Or The Value Of Dowry Given, Whichever Is More.

Defence Against False Dowry Cases

Defending Against False Dowry Cases Involves A Combination Of Legal Strategies And Gathering Evidence. Here Are Some Steps That Can Be Taken:

1. Legal Counsels

• Hiring A Competent Lawyer Who Specializes In Matrimonial Cases Is Crucial. They Can Guide You Through The Legal Process And Help In Building A Strong Defence.

2. Evidence Collection:

- Collect As Much Evidence As Possible To Disprove The Allegations. This Includes Recording All Conversations (Voice, Chat, Email, Letters, Etc.) And Keeping The Originals In A Safe Place.

3. Anticipatory Bail:

- If There's A Risk Of Arrest, Apply For Anticipatory Bail. This Will Prevent Arrest And Allow You To Move Freely And Assist In Your Defence.

4. Witnesses:

- Gather Witness Statements From People Who Can Testify To Your Character And Behaviour, As Well As The Dynamics Of Your Marriage.

5. Documentation:

- Keep A Record Of All Financial Transactions, Especially Those Related To Marriage Expenses, To Counter Claims Of Dowry Demands.

6. Supreme Court Guidelines:

- Familiarize Yourself With The Supreme Court's Guidelines On Handling Dowry Cases To Ensure Your Rights Are Not Violated.

7. Mediation And Settlement:

- Consider Mediation As An Option For Amicable Settlement, Which Can Then Be Presented To The Court To Quash The Allegations.

8. Restitution Of Conjugal Rights (RCR):

- If Applicable, Filing For RCR Can Be A Step To Show The Court Your Willingness To Reconcile And Live With Your Spouse.

9. Avoiding Settlements Under Pressure:

- Do Not Agree To Unfair Settlements Or Demands Under Pressure. Consult With Your Lawyer Before Making Any Decisions.

10. Raising Awareness:

- Educate Yourself About The Laws And Rights To Avoid Being Exploited By False Allegations.

Proving That There Was No Demand Or Acceptance Of Dowry During A Marriage Can Be Challenging, But Here Are Some Strategies That Can Be Used:

1. Communication Records:

-Preserve Any Written Communication Such As Letters, Emails, Text Messages, Or Whatsapp Messages That Indicate No Dowry Demands Or Harassment Were Made.

2. Witness Statements:

- Statements From Witnesses Who Have Firsthand Knowledge Of The Marriage Negotiations And Can Testify That No Dowry Was Demanded Or Accepted.

3. Dowry List:

- If A Dowry List Was Prepared During The Marriage Negotiations, Keeping A Copy Can Help. However, If No Such List Exists, It Can Support The Claim That No Dowry Was Involved.

4. Financial Records:

- Bank Statements, Property Documents, And Other Financial Records Showing That No Transactions Related To Dowry Took Place.

5. Cross-Examination:

- During Legal Proceedings, Cross-Examination Can Be Used To Challenge The Credibility Of The Allegations And To Bring Out The Truth.

6. Affidavits:

- An Affidavit From The Bride's Family Stating That No Dowry Was Given Or Received Can Be A Strong Piece Of Evidence.

7. Marriage Gifts:

- Differentiating Between Customary Marriage Gifts And Dowry Can Help Clarify That What Was Exchanged Does Not Constitute A Dowry.

8. Lack Of Evidence:

- Pointing Out The Absence Of Evidence To Support The Dowry Demand Or Acceptance Can Work In Favor Of The Accused.

The Protection Of Women From Domestic Violence Act

The Protection Of Women From Domestic Violence Act, 2005 Is An Important Legislation Enacted By The Parliament Of India To Safeguard Women From Domestic Violence. Let's Delve Into The Key Aspects Of This Act:

Purpose And Scope:

The Act Aims To Provide More Effective Protection For Women Whose Rights Are Guaranteed Under The Indian Constitution And Who Are Victims Of Any Form Of Violence Occurring Within The Family.

It Addresses Both Recognized And Latent Forms Of Violence Against Women In Domestic Relationships, Whether Within Or Outside Marriage.

Definitions:

Aggrieved Person: Refers To Any Woman Who Is, Or Has Been, In A Domestic Relationship With The Respondent (The Alleged Perpetrator) And Alleges To Have Been Subjected To Any Act Of Domestic Violence.

Child: Includes Any Person Below The Age Of Eighteen Years, Including Adopted, Step, Or Foster Children.

Domestic Relationship: Encompasses A Relationship Between Two Persons Who Live Or Have Lived Together In A Shared Household. This Relationship Can Be Based On Consanguinity, Marriage, Or A Relationship Akin To Marriage.

Reliefs And Orders:

The Act Provides For Various Reliefs And Orders To Protect Aggrieved Women:

Protection Orders: Aimed At Preventing The Respondent From Committing Acts Of Domestic Violence.

Residence Orders: Ensure The Right Of The Aggrieved Person To Reside In The Shared Household.

Monetary Reliefs: Address Financial Needs Arising From Domestic Violence.

Custody Orders: Pertaining To The Custody Of Children.

Compensation Orders: Grant Compensation To The Aggrieved Person.

Interim And Ex Parte Orders: Can Be Issued During Ongoing Proceedings.

Procedure For Obtaining Relief

The Aggrieved Person Can Approach A Magistrate To Seek Relief Under This Act.

The Proceedings Are Held In Camera (Confidentially).

The Act Emphasizes The Right Of The Aggrieved Person To Reside In The Shared Household.

Duties And Responsibilities:

Protection Officers: Appointed To Assist Aggrieved Persons And Ensure Compliance With Orders.

Service Providers: Play A Crucial Role In Providing Support Services.

Government: Has Duties Related To Implementation And Awareness.

Defences In Domestic Violence Cases

Defending Against False Domestic Violence Allegations In India Can Be Challenging, But With The Right Approach And Guidance, You Can Successfully Navigate The Legal Process. By Understanding Domestic Violence Laws, Taking The Appropriate Initial Steps, Working Closely With Your Lawyer, And Keeping In Mind The Expert Tips Provided, You Can Build A Strong Defence And Protect Your Rights. Remember To Stay Calm, Maintain A Record Of Your Interactions, And Rely On The Support Of Your Friends And Family Throughout The Process.

It's Important To Note That The Success Of These Defences Depends On The Specific Circumstances Of Each Case And The Quality Of The Evidence Presented. Legal Representation Is Crucial In Navigating These Complex Situations

Gathering Evidence To Prove Innocence In A Domestic Violence Case Involves Several Steps:

1. Consult A Lawyer:

- Engage A Lawyer Experienced In Handling Domestic Violence Cases To Guide You Through The Legal Process And Build A Strong Defence.

2. Gather Evidence:

- Collect Any Available Evidence That Can Disprove The Allegations, Such As Medical Records, Communication Records, Photographs, Or Witness Statements.

3. File A Counter Complaint:

- If You Have Reason To Believe That The Allegations Are Baseless And Malicious, Consider Filing A Counter Complaint Under Relevant Laws That Deal With False Information Provided With The Intent To Cause Harm.

4. Challenge The Complainant's Evidence:

- Scrutinize The Evidence Presented By The Complainant And Highlight Any Inconsistencies Or Weaknesses In Their Case.

5. Present Your Evidence:

- Submit The Evidence You Have Gathered To Disprove The Allegations And Establish Your Innocence.

6. Cross-Examine Witnesses:

- Cross-Examine The Complainant's Witnesses To Uncover Any Discrepancies In Their Statements Or Reveal Their Potential Bias.

7. Maintain Records:

- Keep A Record Of Any Interactions With The Complainant, Including Phone Calls, Text Messages, Or Emails, To Provide Context And Evidence In Your Defence.

8. Seek Support:

- Reach Out To Friends And Family For Emotional Support And Assistance In Gathering Evidence And Securing Witnesses.

Expert Tips For Defending False Cases

Keep The Following Tips In Mind When Defending Yourself Against False Domestic Violence Allegations:

Stay Calm And Composed: Maintain Your Composure During The Trial And Avoid Emotional Outbursts Or Aggressive Behaviour.

Avoid Direct Contact With The Complainant: Minimize Any Direct Contact With The Complainant, As Any Interaction Could Be Used Against You In Court.

Bigamy:

Bigamy Is Punishable Under Section 494 Of The Indian Penal Code (IPC).

The Punishment For Bigamy Includes Imprisonment For Up To 7 Years And A Fine.

The Second Marriage Is Considered Void If The First Marriage Is Still Valid.

Note: In the Bhartiya Nyaya Sanhita, Bigamy has been defined under section 82

Defending Against A False Bigamy Case Can Be Challenging, But There Are Legal Strategies You Can Consider. Keep In Mind That I Am Not A Lawyer, And It's Essential To Consult With A Legal Professional For Personalized Advice. Here Are Some General Steps You Might Take:

Understand The Allegations:

Carefully Review The Allegations Made Against You. Understand The Specific Claims Related To Bigamy.

Gather All Relevant Documents, Including Marriage Certificates, Divorce Decrees, And Any Other Evidence That Supports Your Case.

Consult An Experienced Attorney:

Seek Legal Representation From An Experienced Criminal Defence Lawyer.

Present Evidence Of Innocence Or Good Faith:

Show That You Did Not Intentionally Commit Bigamy.

Provide Evidence That You Believed Your First Marriage Was Legally Dissolved (If Applicable).

If You Were Misled Or Deceived, Present Evidence To Support This Claim.

Challenge The Validity Of The First Marriage:

If The First Marriage Was Void Or Legally Dissolved, Emphasize This Fact.

Prove That You Had A Reasonable Belief That The First Marriage Was No Longer Valid.

Cross-Examine Witnesses:

Disprove Any False Claims Made By The Complainant.

Question The Credibility Of Witnesses Who Testify Against You.

Prove Lack Of Signature On Marriage Certificate:

If The Marriage Certificate Lacks Your Signature, Highlight This As Evidence.

Show That The Certificate Is Invalid Due To This Discrepancy1.

File A Petition To Quash Proceedings:

Consider Filing A Petition Under Section 482 Of The Code Of Criminal Procedure, 1973.

This Empowers The High Court To Quash Criminal Proceedings Against An Accused.

Things To Be Remembered

Conversion And Bigamy – The Legal Paradox

Conversion To Another Religion Does Not Automatically Dissolve The First Marriage.

Marrying Again After Conversion Without Legally Dissolving The First Marriage Is Still Bigamy.

Live-In Relationships And Bigamy:

Live-In Relationships Are Not Legally Recognized As Marriages.

Bigamy Does Not Apply To Live-In Partners.

Protecting One's Rights During Police Investigations, Especially In Cases Of False Allegations, Is Crucial. Here Are Some Steps That Can Be Taken:

1. Know Your Rights:

- Be Aware Of Your Legal Rights, Such As The Right To Remain Silent And The Right To An Attorney. You Are Not Obligated To Provide Any Information That May Incriminate You.

2. Legal Representation:

- Exercise Your Right To Have A Lawyer Present During Questioning. A Lawyer Can Guide You On What Information You Should And Should Not Disclose.

3. Document Everything:

- Keep Detailed Records Of All Interactions With Law Enforcement, Including Dates, Times, And The Nature Of The Conversations.

4. Avoid Self-Incrimination:

- Do Not Discuss The Case With Anyone Other Than Your Lawyer, As Anything You Say Can Be Used Against You.

5. Preserve Evidence:

- Collect And Preserve Any Evidence That May Help Prove Your Innocence Or Demonstrate The Falsity Of The Allegations.

6. Witnesses:

- Identify Potential Witnesses Who Can Corroborate Your Version Of Events Or Attest To Your Character.

7. Stay Calm And Composed:

- Maintain Composure During Interactions With The Police. Being Argumentative Or Aggressive Can Harm Your Case.

8. Bail:

- If Arrested, Understand The Bail Process And Work With Your Attorney To Secure Your Release While Awaiting Trial.

9. Challenge Illegal Procedures:

- If You Believe Your Rights Have Been Violated During The Investigation, Such As Through An Illegal Search, Inform Your Attorney, Who Can Challenge Such Actions In Court.

10. Seek Dismissal:

- If There Is Compelling Evidence Of Your Innocence, Your Attorney May Be Able To Have The Charges Dismissed Before Trial.

During Police Investigations Related To False Allegations, People May Inadvertently Make Common Mistakes That Can Impact Their Case.

Here Are Some Pitfalls To Avoid:

1. Talking Without Legal Representation:

• One Of The Most Significant Mistakes Is Speaking To The Police Without Legal Counsel. Anything You Say Can Be Used Against You, So It's Crucial To Have An Attorney Present During Questioning

2. Providing Inconsistent Statements:

• Consistency Is Essential. Providing Different Versions Of Events Can Raise Suspicion And Weaken Your Defence. Stick To A Clear And Consistent Narrative.

3. Volunteering Information:

• Avoid Volunteering Unnecessary Information. Answer Questions Directly And Concisely Without Elaborating Unless Advised By Your Lawyer.

4. Admitting Guilt Or Responsibility:

• Never Admit Guilt Or Responsibility During Questioning. Even If You Believe You Are Innocent, Avoid Making Statements That Could Be Misconstrued.

5. Not Documenting Interactions:

• Keep Records Of All Interactions With The Police,

Including Dates, Times, And The Officers' Names. This Documentation Can Be Valuable Later.

6. Agreeing To Searches Without A Warrant

- You Have The Right To Refuse Searches Without A Warrant. Be Aware Of Your Rights And Exercise Them Appropriately.

7. Ignoring Your Right To Remain Silent

- You Have The Right To Remain Silent. Use It. Do Not Feel Pressured To Provide Information That May Incriminate You.

Defending Against Maintenance Cases

Defending Against Maintenance Cases (Such As Alimony Or Spousal Support) Requires A Strategic Approach. Here Are Some Key Defence Strategies:

1. Prove That Maintenance Is Not Required:

- If The Accused Can Demonstrate That Their Spouse Is Not Entitled To Maintenance, They May Be Able To Get The Case Dismissed.

- Evidence Can Include The Spouse's Financial Independence, Maintenance Received From Another Source, Or Proof That The Accused Is Already Providing Maintenance.

2. Challenge The Prima Facie Need For Maintenance:

- Contest The Need For Maintenance By Demonstrating Self-Sufficiency Or Illustrating The Spouse's Capacity For Self-Maintenance.

- Factors To Consider Include Educational Qualifications, Vocational Skills, And Employability.

3. Financial Disclosure:

- Both Parties Should File An Affidavit Of Disclosure Of Assets And Liabilities In All Maintenance Proceedings.

- Transparent Financial Disclosure Helps The Court Determine The Appropriate Amount Of Maintenance.

4. Understand The Criteria For Determining Quantum Of Maintenance:

- The Objective Of Granting Maintenance Is To Prevent The Dependent Spouse From Falling Into Destitution Due To The Failure Of The Marriage. - Factors Considered Include The Status Of The Parties, Reasonable Needs Of The Spouse And Children, Education, Independent Income, And Standard Of Living.

Common Mistakes People Make When Defending Against Maintenance Cases

When Defending Against Maintenance Cases, People May Inadvertently Make Common Mistakes That Can Impact Their Case. Here Are Some Pitfalls To Avoid:

1. Lack Of Legal Representation:

- Not Seeking Legal Counsel Is A Significant Mistake. Engage An Experienced Family Law Attorney Who Can Guide You Through The Legal Process And Build A Strong Defence.

2. Ignoring Court Hearings:

- Failing To Attend Court Hearings Or Cooperating With Legal Proceedings Can Weaken Your Defence. Attend All Hearings And Cooperate With The Process.

3. Inadequate Financial Disclosure:

- Hiding Assets Or Income Can Harm Your Case. Be Transparent About Your Financial Position And Provide Accurate Documentation.

4. Not Challenging The Legitimacy Of The Claim:

- Contest The Grounds On Which Maintenance Is Claimed. If You Can Prove That Maintenance Is Not Required, It May Lead To A Dismissal.

5. Not Cross-Examining Witnesses:

- Cross-Examine Witnesses Presented By The Complainant. This Can Expose Inconsistencies And Weaken Their Arguments.

6. Neglecting Negotiation And Settlement:

- Consider Negotiating And Reaching A Settlement Outside The Court. An Amicable Arrangement Can Be Beneficial.

7. Ignoring Changed Circumstances:

- If There Have Been Significant Changes In Circumstances Since The Maintenance Order Was Issued, Present These Changes To The Court.

8. Not Documenting Efforts To Provide Maintenance:

- If There Are Allegations Of Neglect, Document Instances Where You Have Attempted To Provide Financial Support

Inadequate Financial Disclosure During Legal Proceedings Related To Maintenance Claims Can Have Significant Consequences. Here Are Some Potential Outcomes:

1. Contempt Of Court:

- If A Party Intentionally Withholds Or Misrepresents Financial Information, They May Be Held In Contempt Of Court.

- Contempt Proceedings Can Result In Fines, Penalties, Or Even Imprisonment.

2. Adverse Inferences:

- Courts May Draw Adverse Inferences Against The Party That Fails To Provide Complete And Accurate Financial Disclosure.

- This Can Impact The Court's Decision On Maintenance.

3. Unfair Settlements:

- Inadequate Financial Disclosure Can Lead To Unfair Settlements.

- The Court May Base Its Decision On Incomplete Or Misleading Information.

4. Loss Of Credibility:

- A Party's Credibility Can Suffer If They Are Found To Have Concealed Relevant Financial Details.

- This Can Affect The Court's Perception Of Their Overall Case.

5. Adjustment Of Maintenance Amount:

- If A Party Later Reveals Undisclosed Assets, The Court May Adjust The Maintenance Amount Accordingly.

- The Non-Disclosing Party May End Up Paying More Than They Would Have If They Had Been Transparent Initially.

In Summary, Full And Honest Financial Disclosure Is Essential During Maintenance Proceedings To Ensure Fairness And Uphold The Integrity Of The Legal Process

If You Are Seeking Ways To Avoid Maintenance Payments, Especially In The Context Of Legal Proceedings, Here Are Some Strategies To Consider:

1. Prove Willing Separation:

- If You Can Demonstrate That Your Spouse Is Willingly Living Separately From You, It May Weaken Their Claim For Maintenance.

- Gather Evidence Such As Communication Records, Affidavits, Or Witness Testimony To Support This Argument.

2. Show Financial Independence:

- Prove That Your Spouse Is Financially Independent Or Has Other Sources Of Income.

- If They Are Capable Of Self-Maintenance, It Can Be A Valid Defence Against Maintenance Claims.

3. Engage Legal Representation:

- Consult With An Experienced Family Law Attorney Who Can Guide You Through The Legal Process.

- A Competent Lawyer Can Help Build A Strong Defence And Present Your Case Effectively.

4. Attend Court Hearings:

- Attend All Court Hearings Related To The Maintenance Claim.

- Non-Attendance Or Non-Cooperation Can Have Adverse Consequences.

5. Cross-Examine Witnesses:

- Cross-Examine Any Witnesses Presented By Your Spouse.

- This Can Help Expose Inconsistencies And Weaken Their Arguments.

6. File A Counter-Case:

- If You Have Evidence That The Complaint Is False, Consider Filing A Counter-Case For Defamation Or Perjury Against Your Spouse.

Guiding Light:

Navigating Matrimonial Disputes With Judicial Wisdom

Supreme Court Is Strict On Following Guidelines Before Arrest Under Section 498-A

The Supreme Court Has Ordered To Strictly Follow The Decision Given Earlier By The Apex Court Before The Arrest In Section 498A Related To Harassment Of Women For Dowry Or Other Reasons And Other Cases Punishable With Imprisonment Up To Seven Years.

The Apex Court Had Given Guidelines For This In A Case In 2014. This Is Known As Arnesh Kumar Guidelines. The Supreme Court Has Instructed All The High Courts And Police Chiefs Of The States To Ensure Compliance. For This, All High Courts Will Prepare Guidelines In The Form Of Notifications And Orders. These Will Be Followed By The Sessions Court And Other Courts Related To Criminal Cases. Similarly, DGP In All The States Will Issue Instructions To Follow The Guidelines.

The Supreme Court Gave These Instructions While Overturning An Order Of The Jharkhand High Court In Which The Bail Plea Of The Accused In The Case Of Section 498A Was Rejected.

The Supreme Court Of India Has Indeed Established Strict Guidelines To Prevent The Misuse Of Section 498A Of The Indian Penal Code, Which Deals With Cruelty Against Married Women. These Guidelines Aim To Protect Individuals, Particularly Husbands And Their Families, From False Or Frivolous Allegations Under This Provision. Here Are Some Key Guidelines Established By The Supreme Court:

No Automatic Arrest:

The Supreme Court Has Emphasized That Arrests Under Section 498A Should Not Be Made Automatically Upon The Registration Of A Complaint. Law Enforcement Agencies Are Directed To Conduct A Thorough Investigation And Gather Evidence Before Making Any Arrests.

Necessary Investigation:

Before Effecting Any Arrest, The Police Are Required To Conduct A Preliminary Investigation To Determine The Veracity Of The Complaint. This Includes Recording Statements Of The Complainant, Witnesses, And The Accused, As Well As Collecting Relevant Evidence.

Family Welfare Committees:

To Prevent Arbitrary Arrests, The Supreme Court Has Directed The Establishment Of Family Welfare Committees (Fwcs) At The District Level. These Committees Comprise Social Workers, Counsellors, And Other Professionals Who Assess The Validity Of Complaints Before Recommending Further Action To The Police.

No Arrests In Minor Offenses:

In Cases Where The Offense Is Punishable With Imprisonment For A Term Of Up To Seven Years, The Police Are Directed Not To Make Arrests Immediately. Instead, They Should First Attempt To Resolve The Matter Through Counselling And Mediation.

Applicability Of Section 41 Of Crpc:

The Supreme Court Has Reiterated The Provisions Of Section 41 Of The Code Of Criminal Procedure (Crpc), Which Mandate That Arrests Should Be Made Only When Necessary To Prevent The Commission Of A

Cognizable Offense Or To Ensure The Presence Of The Accused During The Investigation.

Judicial Magistrate's Approval: In Cases Where Arrests Are Deemed Necessary, The Police Must Obtain Prior Approval From A Judicial Magistrate Before Making Any Arrests. This Ensures Judicial Oversight And Prevents Arbitrary Or Unwarranted Arrests.

These Guidelines Are Aimed At Balancing The Interests Of Protecting Women From Domestic Violence With The Need To Prevent The Misuse Of Legal Provisions For Harassment Or Extortion. They Emphasize The Importance Of Conducting A Fair And Impartial Investigation Before Taking Any Coercive Action Against The Accused. It Is Essential For Law Enforcement Agencies And Judicial Authorities To Adhere To These Guidelines To Uphold The Principles Of Justice, Fairness, And Rule Of Law.

No Arrests Should Be Made In Matrimonial Cases Before The 'Cooling Period' Ends: Allahabad High Court

Allahabad High Court Has Given An Important Decision Regarding Section 498A Of Dowry Harassment. The Court Said That In Such Cases, Arrests Should Not Be Made Until The 'Cooling Period' Of Two Months Is Over.

The Allahabad High Court Has Directed The Concerned Authorities That No Arrest Should Be Made Before The Expiry Of The 'Cooling Period' Of Two Months In Cases Of Marital Discord Registered Under Section 498A Of The Indian Penal Code (IPC Act 498A). Further, During This Period, The Case Will Be Immediately Referred To The Family Welfare Committee (FWC) Which Will Try To Resolve The Matrimonial Dispute.

Allahabad High Court Gave Instructions

Section 498A Of The IPC Provides For Punishment For Subjecting A Woman To Cruelty To Her Husband Or His Relatives. Justice Rahul Chaturvedi Passed The Order In The Revision Petition Filed By Mukesh Bansal (Father-In-Law), Manju Bansal (Mother-In-Law) And Sahib Bansal (Husband), Challenging The Dismissal Of Their Discharge Application By The Trial Court. The Court Accepted The Discharge Plea Of The In-Laws, But Rejected The Husband's Plea And Directed Him To Appear In The Lower Court.

Regarding The Misuse Of Section 498A Of The IPC, The Court Said, 'It Is Generally Seen That Every Matrimonial Case Is Blown Out Of Proportion Where Serious Allegations Of Dowry Harassment Are Made Against The Husband And All His Family Members. Allegations Are Made. Nowadays This Is Going On Indiscriminately Due To Which Our Social Fabric Is Being Badly Affected.

The Court Said, "In Metropolitan Cities, Live-In Relationships Are Replacing Our Traditional Marriages. In Fact, The Couple Is Resorting To This To Avoid Getting Into Legal Trouble. If Section 498-A Of The Indian Penal Code Continues To Be Misused In This Manner, Our Age-Old System Of Marriage Will Completely Disappear.

The Court Made It Clear In Its Decision That Only Those Cases Under Section 498-A Of The IPC And Other Sections Of The IPC Will Be Referred To The FWC In Which The Punishment Is Less Than 10 Years But There Is No Physical Injury To The Woman.

Case Title: Mukesh Bansal V State Of UP

In Criminal Revision No. 1126 Of 2022 With 1187 Of 2022 And With 1122 Of 2022

Women Have Unleashed "Legal Terrorism" By Misusing Section 498A IPC: Calcutta HC

Single-Judge Justice Subhendu Samanta Said That Section 498A Was Introduced For The Welfare Of Women But The Same Is Now Being Misused By Filing False Cases.

Laws Are Made For The Protection Of The Individual But When They Are Misused Then The Situation Becomes Serious. Such Questions Keep Being Raised Regarding Section 498A Of IPC. Through This, Along With Eliminating The Evil Of Dowry, The Woman Has Been Provided Protection From Harassment By Her Husband Or His Family Members, But The Case Of The Husband Being Implicated In A False Case Keeps Coming Up. When A Similar Case Came Up, The Court Had To Say That This Is 'Legal Terrorism'. The Matter Came Before The Calcutta High Court. The Court Said That Some Women Have Spread 'Legal Terrorism' By Misusing Section 498A Of The Indian Penal Code.

Mere Complaint Does Not Prove Harassment:

A Husband And His Family Had Appealed To The High Court. The Court Made A Strong Comment On The Husband's Application Challenging The Criminal Cases Filed By His Estranged Wife.

The Court Said That The Provision Of Section 498A Has Been Implemented To Eliminate The Evils Of Dowry From The Society, But It Has Been Seen In Innumerable Cases That Misuse Of This Provision Spreads New Legal Terrorism. Harassment And Torture Falling Within The Definition Of Protection Under Section 498A Cannot Be Proved By The Complainant Alone.

Crime Could Not Be Proven

The Court Found That The Medical Evidence On Record And The Statements Of The Witnesses Could Not Establish Any Offense Against The Man And His Family. A Single Bench Of Justice Subhendu Samant Quashed The Criminal Proceedings Initiated By The Lower Court On The Basis Of The Woman's Complaint.

The Court Said That In Fact The Allegations Made By The Complainant Against The Husband Are Based Only On His Statement. This Is Not Proven By Any Documentary Or Medical Evidence. The Law Allows The Complainant To File A Criminal Complaint, But It Must Be Justified By Solid Evidence.

Case Title: Swapan Kumar Das V. State Of W.B

The Supreme Court Has Dismissed A Dowry Harassment Case Filed By A Woman Against Her In-Laws, Saying The Woman 'Clearly Wants Revenge'. The Court Said That Granting Permission To Continue The Criminal Proceedings Would Amount To Ensuring Injustice. The Bench Said That Considering The Totality Of Facts And Circumstances, Its Opinion Is That The Allegations Levelled Against The Woman's In-Laws Are Not Sufficient And Prima Facie No Case Is Made Out Against Them. The Supreme Court Said, "The Woman Clearly Wants To Take Revenge On Her In-Laws', The Allegations Are So Far-Reaching And Fraudulent That No Reasonable Person Can Conclude That There Is Sufficient Ground To Take Action Against Her. In Such Circumstances, Allowing The Proceedings Against The Appellant To Continue Would Amount To Ensuring Injustice.

The Supreme Court's Decision Came On A Petition Filed Against An Order Of The Madhya Pradesh High Court, Which Had Refused To Quash The Proceedings Against The Woman's Former Male Relatives And Mother-In-Law.

The Supreme Court Accepted The Appeal Of Abhishek And Others Against The Order Of Madhya Pradesh High Court And Cancelled The FIR Lodged Against Them On Behalf Of His Sister-In-Law Bhavna.

Criminal Appeal No. 1457 Of 2015

The Case Filed By The Daughter-In-Law Got Overturned In The Court.

Women Are Misusing Domestic Violence Law

A Case Of Domestic Violence Was Overturned As Soon As It Reached The Court, In Which The Daughter-In-Law Had Filed A Case Of Domestic Violence Against Her Mother-In-Law, Father-In-Law, Brother-In-Law, Sister-In-Law And Sister-In-Law. When The Hearing Took Place In The Court, The Matter Was Completely Overturned. Commenting On This, The Court Said That Women Are Misusing The Domestic Violence Law. Actually, The House Where This Woman Was Living With Her Husband Was In The Name Of Her Elderly Father-In-Law, But The Mother-In-Law And Father-In-Law Were Living In A Rented House. Commenting On This Attitude Of The Daughter-In-Law, The Court Of Additional Sessions Judge Arun Sukhija Of Karkardooma Court Said That The Supreme Court Has Already Defined The Domestic Violence Act And Made It Clear That This Law Protects Against Atrocities On Women Within The Four Walls Of The House. Will Give Protection.

The Surprising Thing In This Case Was That The Complainant Woman And Her Husband Were Ordered By The Senior Citizens Maintenance And Welfare Tribunal To Vacate The House Of The Elderly Mother-In-Law And The Entire Case Of Domestic Violence Was Against The Elderly Mother-In-Law. This Was Done With The Aim Of Maintaining Possession Of The Father-In-Law's House.

The Supreme Court Had Also Recently Said In A Case That Women Are Using This Law For Financial Gain. The Court Said That In This Case Also The Facts Showed That This Woman Was Not A Victim Of Domestic Violence. Rather, He Had Misused The Law Of Domestic Violence To Gain Control Over His In-Laws' Property. The Court Said That In Fact, When The Mother-In-Law And Father-In-Law Do Not Live Under The Same Roof, Then How Could They Harass Her.

Court Must Scrutinize Wife's FIR To Determine If Allegations Are 'Case Of Clever Drafting' Or Have Some Element Of Truth: Delhi High Court

Delhi High Court In One Of Its Orders Said That The Court Should Investigate The Wife's Complaint Or FIR Against The Husband And His Family Whether It Is A 'Case Of Cheer Drafting' Or Indeed There Is Some Truth In It.

Justice Naveen Chawal Said That Where The Wife Intends To Implicate Her Husband's Entire Family In A Criminal Case, Then It Is Possible That She Will Prepare A Complaint Through Her Lawyer Making Specific Allegations Against Everyone. If This Happens, The Entire Family Of The Husband Will Have To Suffer The Pain Of Litigation, Which Will Defeat The Ends Of Justice.

Justice Said That It Is Therefore Necessary That The Court Should Investigate The Wife's Complaint/FIR To See Whether The Allegations Made Are Cleverly Prepared Or There Is Some Truth In Them. He Also Said That The Court Is Not Expected To Hold A Hearing On This Matter, But In Such A Situation It Cannot Remain A Silent Spectator. If He Feels That By Continuing The Court Proceedings The Ends Of Justice Would Be Defeated And The Accused Would Be Subjected To Unnecessary Harassment, Agony And Pain. Apart From This, If The Criminal Process Is Misused Then It Cannot Refuse To Exercise Its Right To Quash The Case.

With The Above Comment, The Court Quashed The FIR Lodged By A Wife In The Year 2017 Against Her Husband's Maternal Uncle And Aunt Under Sections 498 A, 406 And 34 Of The Indian Penal Code.

In The Said Case, The Husband's Maternal Uncle And Aunt Had Filed A Petition Seeking Quashing Of The FIR On The Ground That They Were Living Separately From The Husband And Wife And They Were Dragged Into The Case Only Because They Were Members Of The Husband's Family.

Case Title: Rajesh Aggarwal And Anr. V State NCT Of Delhi And Anr.

Husband Seeking Money From Wife's Parents To Support Child Not Dowry Demand: Patna High Court

Patna High Court Has Given An Important Provision Regarding The Definition Of Dowry. The High Court, While Hearing A Dowry Harassment Case, Has Said That The Amount Demanded From The In-Laws For The Upbringing Of The Child Will Not Fall In The Category Of Dowry.

If A Person Demands Money From His Wife Or In-Laws Before Or After Marriage, Then It Comes Under The Category Of Dowry. There Is A Provision Of Punishment In The Law For Those Who Demand Dowry. But Patna High Court Gave An Important Decision In A Case Related To Dowry. The High Court Has Given An Important Decision Saying That If The Husband Demands Money From The Wife's Ancestral House For The Upbringing Of His Newborn Child, Then Such Demand Does Not Come Under The Definition Of Dowry. A Single Bench Of Justice Bibek Chaudhary Gave This Decision While Accepting The Criminal Revision Petition Filed By Naresh Pandit. The Petitioner Had Challenged His Sentence In The High Court Under Section 498A Of The IPC And Section 4 Of The Dowry Prohibition Act 1961.

The Court Was Told That The Marriage Of Petitioner Naresh With Srijan Devi Took Place In The Year 1994 As Per Hindu Customs. During This Time, They Had Three Children – Two Boys And A Girl. The Wife Alleged That Three Years After The Birth Of Their Daughter, The Petitioner Demanded Rs 10,000 From Her Father For The Care And Maintenance Of The Girl. It Was Also Alleged That The Wife Was Tortured When Her

Demands Were Not Met. After Examining The Case, The Court Found That The Demand Of Rs 10,000 Was Not Made As Consideration For The Marriage Between The Complainant And The Petitioner, Hence, It Does Not Fall Within The Definition Of 'Dowry' Under Section 498A Of The IPC.

In The High Court, The Lawyer Of Husband Naresh Pandit Had Argued That The Allegations Made By The Wife Against The Husband And Other Accused Persons Of The Family Are Of General And All-Embracing Nature And Hence Their Punishment Order Should Be Cancelled. After Hearing All The Parties, The High Court Cancelled The Verdict And Order Of Conviction And Sentence Passed By The Lower Court. The Court Said That If The Husband Demands Money From The Wife's Ancestral Home For The Upbringing And Maintenance Of His Newborn Child, Then Such Demand Does Not Fall Within The Scope Of The Definition Of Dowry As Per The Dowry Prohibition Act-1961.

Naresh Pandit Vs State Of Bihar & Anr.

Criminal Revision No.1021 Of 2016

Wife's Conduct Of Attempting Suicide, Trying To Put Blame On Husband And His Family Amounts To Cruelty: Delhi High Court Upholds Divorce

The Court Said That Due To Such Conduct, The Husband And His Family Would Be In Constant Danger Of Being Implicated In False Cases.

The Delhi High Court Recently Said That A Wife Attempting Suicide And Then Trying To Blame Her Husband And In-Laws Is An Act Of Extreme Cruelty And Grounds For Divorce. A Division Bench Of Justices Suresh Kumar Kait And Neena Bansal Krishna Said Such Conduct Would Expose The Husband And His Family To The Constant Risk Of Being Implicated In False Cases.

"Such Conduct Of The Appellant In Attempting Suicide And Then Trying To Blame The Husband And His Family Members Is An Act Of Extreme Cruelty As The Family Is Being Constantly Threatened With Being Implicated In False Cases," The Court Said.

Therefore, The Bench Dismissed The Appeal Filed By A Woman Challenging A Family Court Order Divorcing Her Husband On The Grounds Of Cruelty.

In This Case, The Couple Got Married In The Year 2007 And A Child Was Born Out Of The Marriage. However, The Husband Alleged That The Wife Left Her In-Laws After Only Four Months Of Marriage.

It Was Said That She Lodged A Complaint With The Police That A Huge Amount Of Dowry Was Given And More Was Being Demanded By The Husband's Parents.

The Court Was Told That In December 2009 The Wife Had Also Tried To Commit Suicide By Consuming Mosquito Repellent Liquid.

After Considering The Allegations, The Bench Said That Even Though The Wife Had Claimed That She Was Forced To Write The Suicide Note, In Her Cross-Examination She Admitted That Her Husband Was At Home When She Attempted To Commit Suicide. Neither Was There.

The Bench Further Said That The Wife Had Filed Several Complaints And Even Though She Was Acquitted In Many Such Cases, She Continued To File Appeals To Ensure That She And Her Family Members Were Put In Jail.

The Court Said, "There Is No Doubt That The Appellant Has A Legal Right To Seek Recourse For Wrongdoing, But Making Baseless Allegations Of Being Subjected To Dowry Demands Or Acts Of Cruelty By The Respondent Or Her Family Members And Against The Respondent Initiating Criminal Prosecution Is Clearly An Act Of Cruelty.

The Court Ultimately Concluded That In This Case, During The Two Years Of Their Marital Life, The Parties Lived Together For Barely Ten Months And Even During That Time, There Were Various Acts Of Cruelty, Including Initiation Of False Complaints, Sexual Harassment Of The Husband, Civil And Criminal Suits Brought By The Per-Wife Were Included.

The High Court Said, "Therefore, We Conclude That The Additional Chief Justice Of The Family Court Has Rightly Held That The Respondent Was Subjected To Cruelty By The Appellant And Is Entitled For Divorce Under Section 13(1)(IA) Of The Hindu Marriage Act. Was Given.

MAT.APP. (F.C.) 37/2022 & CM APPL.16702/2022

Conviction In Dowry Case Is Less Than One Percent

In The Country's Capital Delhi, The Conviction Rate Of The Accused In Dowry Harassment Cases Is Less Than 1%. During The Last Two And A Half Years, Only 0.94% Of The Accused Have Been Convicted In Dowry Harassment Cases, While The Number Of Accused Who Are About To Be Tried Is Above One Thousand.

According To Court Records, Between January 1, 2021 And June 30, 2023, The Allegation Of Dowry Harassment Has Been Proved In Only Five Cases, Whereas After Years Of Dowry Harassment Trials, About 1200 Accused Have Been Acquitted In 527 Cases. In These Cases, Apart From The Husband, Other In-Laws Were Also Made Accused By The Victim's Side, But The Allegations Against Them Could Not Be Proved. In The Five Cases In Which The Charges Have Been Proved, 11 People From The In-Laws' Side Have Been Punished. In Most Of The Cases, It Has Also Come To Light That The Victim Herself Has Retracted Her Statement. The Court Has Accepted That Due To Lack Of Solid Grounds, There Is No Other Option Other Than Acquitting The Accused In Dowry Harassment Cases.

Domestic Disputes Turned Into Dowry Harassment

In A Separate Case, The Victim Told The Dwarka Court That She Often Had Fights With Her Brother-In-Law. The Husband Also Spoke On Behalf Of His Brother-In-Law. One Day Brother-In-Law Raised His Hand On Her. She Angrily Reached Thane To Lodge A Complaint. Instead Of A Fight, The Police Registered The Case As Dowry Harassment. Later, On The Basis Of The Statement Of The Victim, The In-Laws Were Acquitted By The Court.

Same Is The Situation In The Entire Country Regarding Matrimonial Disputes, Most Of The Cases Are Presented In The Court By The Police Or Lawyers In A Big Way.

Single Event May Not Be Enough To Prove Cruelty: Supreme Court

The Supreme Court Made Important Comments In The Case Of Cruelty Allegations And Conviction. The Top Court Said, A Mere Example Cannot Be Sufficient To Implicate A Person In The Crime Of Cruelty. The Court Also Laid Down The Condition That The Cruelty Must Be Extraordinary.

The Supreme Court Has Made Important Comments Regarding The Allegations Of Cruelty And Proving Guilt Before The Court. Regarding The Allegations Of The Married Woman, The Top Court Said That A Mere Example Cannot Be Enough To Implicate A Person In The Crime Of Cruelty. The Court Also Laid Down The Condition That The Example Of Cruelty Should Be Obvious And Extraordinary. Four People Got Relief From This Decision Of The Court. In This Case Of Dowry Harassment And Cruelty, The Court Quashed The Criminal Proceedings Against Four People, Including The Sister And Cousins Of The Accused Person.

In The Supreme Court, A Bench Of Justice Sanjiv Khanna And Justice SVN Bhatti Said, In A Case Of Cruelty To A Married Woman, Cruelty Cannot Be Proved In The Absence Of Physical Evidence Of Involvement Of The Accused. The Court Said, Unless The Allegations And Evidence Are Clear, They Cannot Be Considered Sufficient To Implicate Someone Under Charges Of Cruelty. Regarding Marital Cruelty Of The Complainant, The Court Said The Claims Against The Petitioners Seeking Relief Were Found To Be "Very Vague And General" In Nature.

The Apex Court Granted Relief To The Accused For Allegedly Committing Offenses Under Sections 498A And 506 Of The Indian Penal Code (IPC) And Provisions Of The Dowry Prohibition Act, 1961. The Supreme Court

Said, In The Absence Of Any Material Evidence Of Interference And Involvement In The Marital Life Of The Complainant, The Accused Cannot Be Held Guilty Of Cruelty Under Section 498A Of The IPC. The Court, In Its Order Passed On November 30, Said That Unless There Is Clear Evidence And Examples Of Cruelty, The Accused Cannot Be Convicted On This Basis.

The Court, In Its Order, Observed That The Petitioners Seeking Relief From The Charge Of Cruelty Were Not Living In The Matrimonial Home. One Of Them Was Also Living Outside India. Giving Relief To The Accused, The Supreme Court Said, In The Absence Of Specific Details To Prove Cruelty, The Court Allows The Present Appeal. The Top Court Passed This Order On A Petition Challenging The Karnataka High Court Order. In The Order Passed In March 2019, The High Court Had Refused To Quash The Charge Sheet Against The Four Accused.

The Woman Who Complained Of Cruelty Was Married In June 2015. She Had Filed A Complaint Following Which An FIR Was Registered In Karnataka In November 2016. The Woman Had Alleged That In February 2016, One Of The Appellants (In-Laws) Had Allegedly Commented On Her Physical Appearance. The Woman Had Also Made Allegations Of Throwing Personal Belongings In The Dustbin.

Case: Mahalakshmi Vs. State Of Karnataka

CRIMINAL APPEAL NO. 494/2023

Husband Cannot Be Held Guilty Of Abetting Suicide: Supreme Court

In The Absence Of Any Concrete Evidence Of Torture Or Cruelty, An Accused Cannot Be Convicted Under Section 306 Of The IPC By Inference Under Section 113A.

The Supreme Court Has Acquitted A Man Accused Of Abetting His Wife's Suicide Three Decades Ago, Saying A Husband Cannot Be Held Guilty Of Abetting His Wife's Suicide Within Seven Years Of Marriage Unless There Is Strong Evidence Of Harassment Or Cruelty. Section 113A Of The Indian Evidence Act Establishes The Presumption Of Abetment By The Husband And In-Laws In Cases Where The Woman Has Committed Suicide Within Seven Years Of Marriage And Has Been Subjected To Cruelty. Yes. In The Present Case The Accused Person Was Married In 1992. The Prosecution Claimed That Soon After The Marriage, The Accused And His Parents Started Demanding Money As He (The Accused) Wanted To Start A Ration Shop.

According To The Document, On November 19, 1993, The Woman Committed Suicide By Consuming Poison. According To The Prosecution, She Committed Suicide Due To Constant Harassment By Her Husband. The Additional Sessions Judge, Karnal, In 1998 Convicted The Man Of An Offense Punishable Under Section 306 Of The Indian Penal Code (IPC), Who Was Booked In The Punjab And Haryana High Court Upheld. The Top Court Said That To Convict A Person Under Section 306 (Abetment

Of Suicide) Of The Indian Penal Code (IPC), There Must Be Clear 'Criminal Intention' To Commit The Offence.

Justice J. B. A Bench Of Justice Pardiwala And Justice Manoj Mishra Said Mere Harassment Is Not Sufficient To Hold An Accused Guilty Of Abetment Of Suicide And It Also Requires A Direct Act Which Caused The Person To Commit Suicide. The Apex Court Said That The Courts Should Be Very Careful And Cautious In Applying The Correct Principles Of Law To The Subject Of Abetment Of Suicide Of A Woman Within Seven Years Of Marriage, Otherwise The Impression May Be Created That The Conviction Is Not Legal But Moral. The Bench Said That This Court Has Held That The Fact Of Suicide Within Seven Years Of Marriage Should Not Lead One To Conclude The Offense Of Abetment Unless Cruelty Is Proved. In The Absence Of Any Concrete Evidence Of Torture Or Cruelty, An Accused Cannot Be Convicted Under Section 306 Of The IPC By Inference Under Section 113A.

Case Title: Naresh Kumar V. State Of Haryana

Living Separately Is Also Cruelty: Supreme Court

If Husband And Wife Remain Separated For A Long Time Then This Is Also Cruelty. The Supreme Court Has Made This Comment While Hearing A Divorce Case. Considering A Couple's Separation For 25 Years As A Ground For Divorce, The Apex Court Gave Permission To Both Of Them To Break Their Relationship. The Court Said That If A Couple Lives Separately For 25 Years, Then It Is Cruel To Call Them Married. After Marriage, The Couple Lived Together Only For 4 Years And Were Separated Since Then. Justice Sudhanshu Dhulia And Justice J B Pardiwala Said That Ending All Important Relations And Living With Bitterness Should Also Be Considered As Cruelty.

Taking The Hindu Marriage Act As The Basis, The Judges Said That Living Separately For So Many Years Is Not Good For Marriage And Becomes A Reason For Divorce. The Supreme Court Said, "We Have Before Us A Married Couple Who Lived Together Only For 4 Years. After That They Remained Separated And Have Not Been Together For 25 Years. He Does Not Have Any Children From This Marriage. Their Relationship Is Broken In A Way That Cannot Be Repaired. The Court Clearly Said, "We Have No Doubt That This Relationship Should End As Its Continuation Would Be Cruel. Staying Apart For A Long Time And Losing All Important Relationships Is Also Cruel.

Not Only This, The Court Said That The Breakup Of Their Marriage Would Probably Not Make Any Difference To Anyone. This Effect Would Occur Only If They Had Any Children Who Would Be Affected By The Divorce. Apart From This, The Court Ordered The Husband To Provide An Amount Of Rs 30 Lakh To The Woman As Compensation.

The Couple Got Married In 1994 In Delhi. The Husband Alleged That The Wife Had Got The Abortion Done Without Informing Him. She Said She

Didn't Like My House Because It Was Small. Four Years Had Passed Since The Marriage And She Left The House.

The Man Said That His Wife Had Filed A Case Of Dowry Harassment. The Husband And His Brother Were Arrested In This Case, But Were Later Released. After This He Decided To Divorce His Wife. The Trial Court Had Granted Divorce On The Grounds Of Long Separation And Cruelty. However, The Delhi High Court Had Rejected The Divorce Decision, After Which The Man Approached The Supreme Court And Demanded That The Divorce Be Granted.

Case Title: Rakesh Raman V. Kavita

Allegations By Highly Educated Spouse Damaging Reputation, Career Of Partner Amounts To Mental Cruelty Entitling Grant Of Divorce: Supreme Court

The Supreme Court, While Accepting The Ground Of Mental Cruelty For Divorce, Said That The Mental Cruelty Should Be To Such An Extent That It Has Become Impossible For The Spouses To Live Together And Lead A Married Life. However, The Limit Of Tolerance May Be Different For Every Couple.

The Supreme Court Has Said In An Important Decision On Friday That It Is Mental Cruelty For A Highly Educated Person To Spoil The Reputation And Career Of His Spouse And Cause Irreparable Harm To Her. The Court Considered The Wife's Behaviour As Mental Cruelty And Accepted The Husband's Divorce Petition.

The Bench Of Justice Sanjay Kishan Kaul, Justice Dinesh Maheshwari And Justice Hrishikesh Rai Accepted The Husband's Petition, Quashed The Decision Of The Uttarakhand High Court And Reinstated The Decision Of The Family Court To Grant The Divorce Decree. The Supreme Court Said That It Is Wrong For The High Court To Call Broken Relationships A Part Of The Married Life Of The Middle Class. This Case Is Definitely One Of Cruelty By The Wife Towards Her Husband And The Husband Is Entitled To Get Divorce On This Basis.

Uniform Standards Cannot Be Set: Supreme Court

The Supreme Court, While Accepting The Ground Of Mental Cruelty For Divorce, Said That The Mental Cruelty Should Be To Such An Extent That It Has Become Impossible For The Spouses To Live Together And Lead A

Married Life. However, The Limit Of Tolerance May Be Different For Every Couple. The Bench Said That The Court Should Keep In Mind The Level Of Education And Status Of The Parties While Deciding The Case Of Divorce On The Grounds Of Mental Cruelty. The Bench Said That In The Earlier Judgment Of Samar Ghosh, The Court Had Given Examples Of Mental Cruelty, However, It Had Also Said That No Uniform Standard Can Be Set In This Regard, It Will Be Decided On The Basis Of Each Case.

Wife Had Filed Complaints Against Husband

The Bench Said That In The Present Case The Wife Had Made Several Abusive Complaints Against The Husband To Senior Army Officers. For Which The Army Conducted A Court Of Inquiry Against The Husband. This Affected Her Husband's Progress And Career. Not Only This, The Wife Also Sent A Complaint Against The Husband To Many Other Authorities Such As The State Women's Commission. Posted Derogatory Material Against Her Husband On Other Platforms Also. The Result Was That The Reputation And Career Of The Petitioner Husband Was Affected.

Husband's Career & Reputation Suffered Irreparable Damage.

The Court Said That When The Husband Has Suffered Adverse Effects In His Life And Career Due To The Allegations Made By The Wife, Then The Wife Will Have To Face The Legal Consequences. She Cannot Get Away Just Because No Court Has Found The Allegations To Be False. The High Court's Approach Of Looking At And Deciding The Case Is Not Correct. The Supreme Court Said That In This Case It Will Only Be Seen Whether The Wife's Behaviour Amounts To Mental Cruelty Or Not. In This Case, The Highly Educated Spouse Has Levelled Allegations Against Her Partner, Causing Irreparable Damage To Her Career And Reputation. When Someone's Reputation Among His Colleagues, Superiors And Society Has Been Tarnished, The Affected Person Cannot Be Expected To Forgive His Conduct. It Is Not Justified For The Wife To Say That She Had Made All These Complaints To Save Her Married Life. The Court Said That The

Wronged Party Cannot Expect The Marital Relationship To Continue. The Husband Is Justified In Demanding Separation From Her.

This Was The Whole Matter

In This Case, The Husband Was A Military Officer With An Mtech Degree And The Wife Taught In A Government PG College With A Phd Degree. Both Of Them Got Married In 2006. They Lived Together For A Few Months And Then Had A Falling Out. Both Are Living Separately Since One Year Of Marriage. In This Case The Husband Filed An Application In The Family Court And Asked For Divorce. The Husband Said That His Wife Made Many Complaints Against Him, Made Allegations Against Him Which Caused Damage To His Reputation And Career. This Behaviour Of The Wife Is Mental Cruelty And Hence She Should Be Divorced. Whereas The Wife Filed A Petition Demanding Restoration Of Marital Relations From The Court. The Family Court Had Accepted The Husband's Divorce Petition Considering The Facts And Evidence Of The Case. But The High Court Had Overturned The Decision Of The Family Court Granting Divorce And Accepted The Wife's Demand For Restoration Of Marital Relations.

Case Title: Joydeep Majumdar Vs Bharti Jaiswal Majumdar

Wife Making Serious Allegations Of Criminal Conduct Against Her Husband And His Parents, Which She Was Unable To Prove In The Trial Court, Is An Act Of "CRUELTY":

Delhi High Court

The Division Bench Of Justice Vipin Sanghi And Justice Jasmeet Singh Upheld The Divorce Decree Given By The Family Court In Favor Of The Husband And Dismissed The Appeal Filed By The Wife Under Section 19 Of The Family Court Act.

The Delhi High Court Has Dissolved The Marriage Of A Couple Who Had Been Separated For 12 Years, Saying The Wife Had Filed A Baseless Criminal Complaint Against The Husband And His Family Members, Causing Extreme Mental Cruelty And Suffering To Her.

The Bench Held That There Was No Scope For Reconciliation Between The Parties And The Marriage Had Completely Broken Down. The Court Also Noted That No Useful Purpose Would Be Served By Maintaining This Marital Bond And The Insistence On Continuing The Relationship Would Lead To Further Cruelty To Both The Parties.

The Court Said That,

"At Present The Marital Discord Between The Parties Is Such That Trust, Confidence, Understanding And Mutual Love Has Completely Ended Between Them. The Conduct Of The Respondent (Wife) Has Been Such That It Is Causing Great Mental Anguish To The Appellant (Husband) And The Parties Can No Longer Be Expected To Live With Each Other."

The Court Was Considering An Appeal Challenging The Judgment And Decree Passed By The Family Court In This Case. Before The Family Court, The Appellant Husband Had Filed A Petition Seeking Divorce Under Sections 13(1)(Ia) And 13(1)(Ib) Of The Hindu Marriage Act, 1955. Which Was Rejected By The Family Court.

The Court Said That The Conduct Of The Appellant Shows That, At Least, Till The Time He Filed The Petition Under Section 9 Of The Hindu Marriage Act, 1955, He Wanted To Save The Marriage. However, It Was Noted That The Wife Did Not Resume Living With Him Or Engage With The Husband In Marital Relations.

"Instead, The Respondent Filed A Complaint Before The CAW Cell Alleging Dowry Demands, Threats To Life, And Harassment At The Hands Of The Appellant And His Family Members. The Same Allegations Were Repeated In The Reply To The Petition Filed Under Section 9, Where A Copy Of The Complaint Filed Before The CAW Cell Was Also Attached. The Respondent Also Prayed For Dismissal Of The Petition Filed Under Section 9 Of The Hindu Marriage Act, 1955.

The Court Held That The Wife's Conduct Demonstrated Not Only Her Clear Intention To Leave Her Husband, But Also Her Lack Of Sensitivity Towards The Husband's Physical And Emotional Needs.

'After Almost Two Years Of Leaving The Matrimonial Home And Three Years Of Marriage, The Respondent Committed Dowry Demand, Ill-Treatment, Physical And Mental Torture And Harassment Against The Appellant And Her Family Members On 10.10.2011 At The CAW Cell, Krishna Nagar, Delhi. Filed A Complaint Alleging Other Cruelties. Whereas These Allegations Remained Baseless.

The Court Held That The Allegations Were Not Founded And Amounted To Clear Character Assassination Of The Husband As Well As His Family Members.

Noting That The Family Court Ignored The Said Aspect Of The Case,

"Furthermore, The Appellant Had To Make 30-40 Visits To The Police Station In Connection With The Said Complaint," The Court Said. A Police Station Is Not The Best Place For Anyone To Be. Whenever He Had To Go To The Police Station, He Would Have Suffered Mental Torture And

Trauma. There Was A Sword Of Danger Hanging Over His Head, And He Did Not Know When A Case Would Be Registered Against Him And He Would Be Arrested. As Far As The Respondent Is Concerned, He Had Done Everything To Implicate The Appellant And His Family In The Criminal Case. The Same Prayer Was There In His Complaint Also.

Further, The Court Also Held That The Wife Could Not Justify Her Non-Return To The Matrimonial Home And Her Refusal To Live With The Husband Was Sufficient To Establish Desertion By Her.

The Court Said That,

"In This Case, We Are Of The View That The Appellant Has Been Able To Make Out A Case Of Cruelty And Abandonment By The Respondent. We Are Unable To Agree With The Findings Of The Family Court. The Appellant Is Entitled To Succeed On Both The Grounds I.E. Sections 13(1)(Ia) And 13(1)(Ib).

MAT.APP. (F.C.) 247/2019

It Is Not Cruelty To Live With Another Woman When The Wife Lives Separately: Delhi HC

The Delhi High Court, In An Order, Made It Clear That A Husband Living With Another Woman For A Long Time After Separation From His Wife, When There Is No Possibility Of Reunion, Cannot Be Termed As Cruelty.

A Division Bench Of Justices Suresh Kumar Kait And Neena Bansal Krishna Held That After So Many Long Years Of Separation With No Possibility Of Reunion, The Husband Can Find Solace By Living With Another Woman And This Will Not Deprive Him Of Divorce From His Wife. Can Do.

The Court Observed, "Even If It Is Assumed That During The Pendency Of The Divorce Petition The Respondent-Husband Has Started Living With Another Woman And Has Two Sons, This In Itself Does Not Amount To Cruelty In The Specific Circumstances Of This Case." It Can Be Said That When Both The Parties Are Not Living Together Since 2005, With No Possibility Of Reunion After So Many Long Years Of Separation, The Respondent Husband May Find His Peace And Comfort By Living With Another Woman. But This Is A Subsequent Incident During The Pendency Of The Divorce Petition And The Husband Cannot Be Denied Divorce From The Wife On The Ground Of Proven Cruelty."

It Said The Consequences Of Such A Relationship Would Have To Be Borne By The Defendant-Husband, Woman And Children.

The Court Dismissed A Plea By A Woman Challenging A Family Court Order Divorcing Her Husband On The Grounds Of Cruelty Under Section 13(1)(IA) Of The Hindu Marriage Act, 1955.

The Couple Were Married On 3 December 2003 But Soon Disputes Arose And They Separated In 2005.

It Was Alleged That The Wife Created Many Problems And Subjected Her Husband To Cruelty And Even Got Him Beaten By Her Brother And Relatives. It Was Reported That The Wife And Her Family Members Have Also Been Convicted For The Offense Under Section 506 (II) Of The Indian Penal Code (IPC).

The Appellant-Wife Argued That They Had A Grand Marriage And Yet The Husband Made Several Demands. She Said That Her Mother-In-Law Had Given Her Some Medicines With The Assurance That A Son Would Be Born, But The Purpose Was To Abort Her Pregnancy.

After Considering The Case, The Court Said That Even Though The Wife Had Claimed That She Was Subjected To Harassment And Cruelty For Dowry, She Could Not Prove Her Claim And It Amounted To An Act Of Cruelty.

The Court Said That It Was In The Appeal Itself That The Woman Had Claimed For The First Time That Her Husband Had Married And Given Birth To Two Sons. However, The Bench Said That Neither Any Specific Details Nor Any Evidence Of The Alleged Second Marriage Has Been Produced On Record Or Given In The Complaints Given To The Police.

Therefore, The Court Dismissed The Appeal And Upheld The Trial Court's Order Granting Divorce.

MAT.APP. (F.C.) 236/2018 & CM APPL. 38556/2018

Questioning Husband's Masculinity Is Mental Cruelty & Harassment: Delhi High Court

The Delhi High Court Has Said That Allegations Made By A Wife About A Husband's "Manliness" Can Be Mentally Painful And Contribute To Mental Cruelty.

The Court Said In A Strong Tone That A Woman Accusing Her Husband Of Having An Affair With An Office Lady Is No Less Than Mental Cruelty. The Court Further Said That If A Woman Questions The Masculinity Of Her Husband, Calls Him Impotent And Forces Him To Undergo Medical Tests, That Also Amounts To Mental Cruelty. A Bench Of Justices Suresh Kumar Kait And Neena Bansal Krishna Said The Demand For Dowry, Forcing The Husband To Undergo An Impotence Test Along With Allegations Of Extramarital Affairs And Labelling Him A Womanizer Was Enough To Cause Mental Agony.

Regarding This Matter, The Court Concluded That Making Reckless, Defamatory And Baseless Allegations That Publicly Tarnish The Image Of A Spouse Is An Act Of Extreme Cruelty. The Judgment Came In Response To An Appeal Filed By A Woman Challenging A Family Court's Decision To Divorce Her Husband On The Grounds Of Cruelty.

Know The Matter

The Couple, Who Married In 2000, Have A Son, But Disputes Arose From The Beginning. The Husband Alleged That The Wife Made False Allegations Including Dowry Demands, Extramarital Affairs And Impotence. The Wife Challenged These Claims. The Court, Considering The Evidence, Found That The Husband Was The Victim Of Acts Of Cruelty, Entitling Him To Divorce Under The Hindu Marriage Act. The

Judgment Emphasized The Impact Of Such Allegations On Mental Health And Condemned Public Harassment And Humiliation Within Marriage.

Husband Had To Worry

The Delhi High Court Said, "Unfortunately, Here Is A Case Where The Husband Has Been Publicly Harassed, Humiliated And Verbally Attacked By His Wife. The Woman Who Accused Her Husband Had Even Gone To The Extent Of Accusing Him Of Infidelity In Front Of Office Staff/Guests During Office Meetings. He Even Started Harassing The Female Staff In His Office And Left No Stone Unturned In Portraying Him As A Womanizer In The Office. "This Behaviour Is An Act Of Extreme Cruelty Towards The Respondent/Husband."

Saurabh Jain V. Neha Jain

Taunting Wife About Cooking Is Not 'Cruelty', Bombay High Court Cancels FIR Lodged Against Husband's Relatives

The Wife Had Alleged In Her Complaint That Her Husband's Brothers

Used To Taunt And Insult Her By Saying That She Did Not Know How To Cook And Her Parents Did Not Teach Her Anything.

Commenting On Wife's Cooking Is Not Cruelty Under Section 498A Of IPC. This Is What The Bombay High Court Has To Say. In Fact, The Husband's Relatives Would Taunt The Wife That She Did Not Know How To Cook Properly. Against This The Woman Filed An FIR Against Her Husband's Relatives. And Said That This Is Cruelty Under Section 498A Of IPC. However, Bombay High Court Ordered To Cancel The FIR.

The Wife Had Alleged In Her Complaint That Her Husband's Brothers Used To Taunt And Insult Her By Saying That She Did Not Know How To Cook And Her Parents Did Not Teach Her Anything. The Woman Had Claimed That She Was Thrown Out Of Her In-Law's House In November 2020, After Which She Lodged An FIR On January 9, 2021. After Which The Accused Approached The Court To Cancel The FIR.

What Did The High Court Say?

The Division Bench Of Justice Anuja Prabhudesai And Justice NR Borkar Was Hearing The Case. The Bench Heard The Arguments Of Both The Parties, Looked At The Evidence And Said That Comments Like The Wife Not Knowing How To Cook Do Not Amount To Cruelty Under Section 498A.

Said Further,

"In The Case, The Only Allegation Made Against These Petitioners Is That They Had Commented That The Woman Does Not Know How To Cook. "Such Comments Do Not Amount To 'Cruelty' Under Section 498A Of The IPC."

The Court Said That Under Section 498A Of The IPC, Minor Fights Are Not Considered Cruelty. To Prove The Offense Under Section 498A, It Has To Be Established That The Woman Was Subjected To Continuous Cruelty.

Along With This, The High Court Accepted The Petition Of The Relatives And Ordered To Cancel The FIR.

Case Title: Sandesh Madhukar Salunkhe & Anr Vs State Of Maharashtra

CRIMINAL WRIT PETITION NO. 3936 OF 2021

Constant Taunting About Husband's Earnings Is Mental Cruelty: Delhi High Court

The Delhi High Court Has Termed A Wife's Constant Taunting Of Her Husband About His Earnings And Pressurizing Him To Fulfil Crazy Dreams Beyond His Capacity As Tantamount To Mental Cruelty And Said Divorce Is Justified On This Ground.

Delhi High Court Made A Big Comment While Hearing A Divorce Case. The Court Said That The Wife's Constant Taunting About Her Husband's Earnings And Pressurizing Him To Fulfil His Dreams Beyond His Financial Condition Is Mental Cruelty.

If A Wife Does This, It Gives The Husband The Right To Divorce. A Division Bench Of Justices Suresh Kumar Kait And Neena Bansal Krishna Said That The Spouse Should Not Be Constantly Reminded Of His Financial Limitations. Unreasonable Demands Can Create Constant Dissatisfaction, Which Can Lead To Mental Stress.

'Taunting Can Cause Mental Stress To The Husband'

The Bench Of Justices Suresh And Neena Bansal Krishna Said, "A Wife Should Not Be Constantly Reminded Of Her Husband's Financial Limitations. If The Wife Puts Pressure On Her Spouse To Fulfil Big And Fanciful Dreams Which Are Not Within His Financial Reach, It May Put Him Under Mental Stress. This Will Create A Feeling Of Dissatisfaction Between The Two, Which Can Cause Problems In Marital Life. Therefore, People Should Walk Carefully Between Needs, Wants And Desires.

Court Rejected Wife's Petition

The Delhi High Court Was Hearing A Wife's Plea Challenging A Family Court's Order Divorcing Her Husband On The Grounds Of Cruelty,

Which Was Dismissed By The Bench. The Court Considered The Husband's Plea, Which Said That The Wife's Actions, Which Included Forcing Him To Leave The House, Taunting Him About Taking Loans And Refusing To Adjust To Limited Resources, Amounted To Mental Cruelty.

The Court Said, 'Putting Pressure On The Spouse To Fulfil Distant And Whimsical Dreams Which Are Clearly Not Within His Or Her Financial Reach Can Give Rise To A Feeling Of Persistent Dissatisfaction, Which Can Impair Satisfaction With Any Married Life And There Will Be Enough Mental Stress To Destroy The Peace. Noting The Impact On Mental Health Of Constant Bickering And Quarrels, The Court Said That Seemingly Insignificant Incidents, When They Become Dominant Over Time, Can Cause Mental Stress, Leading To Loss Of Marital Bliss For The Spouses. It Becomes Impossible To Maintain The Relationship.

Citing Section 13(1A)(li) Of The Hindu Marriage Act, The Court Said That Relief Under This Section, Granting Divorce For Non-Compliance With The Order Of Restitution Of Conjugal Rights, Is An Absolute Right Of Any Party.. The Court Rejected The Argument That Only The Party In Whose Favour The Compensation Was Granted Could Demand A Divorce. She Said The Language Of The Section Indicates That Either Party Can Avail Of The Remedy In Case Of Non-Compliance. The Bench Upheld The Family Court's Decision, Highlighting The Husband's Mental Stress And Lack Of Restitution Of Conjugal Rights Despite The Court's Order.

MAT. APP. (F.C.) 167/2019 & CM APPL. 30637/2019

Calling Wife 'Ghost', 'Vampire' Is Not Cruelty: Patna High Court Quashes Husband's Conviction Under Section 498A Of IPC

Patna High Court Has Said That A Husband Calling His Wife A 'Ghost' Or 'Vampire' Is Not An Act Of Cruelty.

A Bench Of Justice Bibek Chaudhary Said That In Marital Relations, Especially In Dysfunctional Marital Relations, There Are Incidents Where Both The Husband And Wife Abuse Each Other By Using Foul Language, However, All Such Allegations Amount To "Cruelty". " Do Not Come Within The Scope Of. ,

The Court Made These Observations While Quashing The Conviction Of A Husband Under Section 498A Of The IPC And Section 4 Of The Dowry Prohibition Act 1961.

The Court Allowed The Revision Petition Filed By The Husband Challenging The Order Of The Additional Sessions Judge, Bihar Sharif, Upholding The Order Of His Conviction Passed By The Chief Judicial Magistrate, Nalanda.

High Court's Comments

At The Outset, The Court Rejected The Argument That The Husband Had Subjected His Wife To Cruelty Just By Calling Her A 'Ghost' And 'Vampire'. The Court Also Observed That Although The Wife In Her

Evidence Stated That She Had Informed Her Father About The Torture Through Several Letters, However, Not A Single Letter Was Produced By The Actual Complainant During The Hearing Of The Case.

The Court Also Said That No Document Was Produced To Show That The Petitioners Had Personally Demanded The Maruti Car And When Such Demand Was Not Met, The Wife (Actually The Daughter Of The Complainant) Was Subjected To Cruelty. The Court Also Took Into Account The Fact That No Specific Allegations Were Made Against The Husband Or His Family Members.

In View Of This, The Court Held That The Case Under Section 498A Of The Indian Penal Code Was The Result Of Personal Grudge And Differences Between The Two Parties. In This Background, The Court Quashed The Order Of Conviction And Allowed The Revision Petition.

CRIMINAL REVISION No.923 Of 2018

Not Marrying After Proposal Is Not Cheating Unless There Is Intention To Cheat: Supreme Court

The Court Said That There May Be Many Reasons For A Marriage Proposal Not Being Materialised, But It Cannot Attract The Offense Of Fraud Unless There Is Evidence To Prove That Fraud Was Intended.

The Supreme Court Recently Quashed A Case Of Cheating Under Section 417 Of The Indian Penal Code (IPC) Against A Person (Petitioner/Appellant) Who Refused To Marry The Girl Despite Negotiating With Her Family To Marry Him. [Raju Krishna Shedbalkar Vs. State Of Karnataka And Others].

A Bench Of Justices Sudhanshu Dhulia And Prasanna B Varale Said There Could Be A Number Of Reasons For A Marriage Proposal Not Materialising, But Unless There Is Evidence To Prove That There Was An Intention To Deceive From The Very Beginning, It There Cannot Be A Crime Of Fraud.

The Court Said "There May Be A Number Of Reasons For Initiating A Marriage Proposal And Then The Proposal Not Reaching The Desired End. In A Given Case It May Involve Fraud; It Is Still Theoretically Possible, In Such Cases, To Commit The Offense Of Fraud To Prove, The Prosecution Must First Have Credible And Reliable Evidence To Prosecute Such A Case. There Is No Such Evidence Before The Prosecution And Hence No Offense Under Section 417 Is Made Out."

The Court Was Hearing An Appeal Filed By The Petitioner Against The July 2021 Order Of The Karnataka High Court, Which Had Quashed The Case Against Other Members Of The Petitioner's Family But Refused To Quash The Case Against Him.

The Case Arises Out Of A Complaint Lodged By The Woman, Who Alleges That The Petitioner Has Cheated Her By Not Marrying Her.

According To The Complaint, She Was Working As A Lecturer When Her Family Was Looking For A Suitable Groom And The Petitioner Was Selected As A Potential Match.

After This, Both Of Them Started Talking To Each Other On The Phone And The Woman's Father Also Gave An Advance Of Rs 75,000 To The Marriage Hall.

However, The Marriage Could Not Take Place When She Learned From A Newspaper Report That The Petitioner Had Married Someone Else.

Thereafter She Lodged A Complaint Against Six Persons Including The Petitioner And Filed An FIR Against Them Under Sections 406 (Criminal Breach Of Trust), 417 (Cheating) And 420 (Fraudulent And Dishonestly Inducing Delivery Of Property) Of The Indian Penal Code. Went.

The Accused Persons Then Moved The High Court Under Section 482 Of The Code Of Criminal Procedure To Quash The Case.

The High Court Quashed The FIR Against All The Accused In Respect Of Offenses Under Sections 406 And 420. With Regard To Section 417, The High Court Concluded That The Same Had Been Done Against The Petitioner, Though Not Against Other Accused Persons.

After This The Petitioner Moved The Supreme Court For Relief.

The Court, After Examining The Relevant Provision And Case Laws, Held That To Attract The Offense Of Fraud, There Must Be An Intention To Deceive Or Defraud From The Very Beginning.

In This Case, The Complaint Itself Did Not Show That The Man Had Such Intent.

Therefore, It Quashed The Criminal Case Against The Petitioner.

CRIMINAL APPEAL NO.577 OF 2024 (ARISING OUT OF SLP (CRL.) NO. 6137 OF 2021)

Property Purchased In Wife's Name Is Family Property: Allahabad High Court

While Hearing The Petition, Allahabad High Court Said That Unless It Is Proved That The Property Has Been Purchased From The Wife's Income, The Property Purchased In The Name Of The Wife Is The Property Of The Family.

The Allahabad High Court Has Held In A Property Dispute That Property Purchased In The Name Of A Housewife Wife Is Family Property As She Has No Independent Source Of Income. While Giving The Above Ruling, Justice Arun Kumar Singh Deshwal Said That It Is Common For Hindu Husbands To Buy Property In The Name Of Their Wives.

The High Court Heard The Petition Filed Regarding The Son's Claim Of Co-Ownership Of His Late Father's Property. Said That The Court Can Hold Under Section 114 Of The Indian Evidence Act That The Property Purchased By A Hindu Husband In The Name Of His Housewife Wife Will Be The Property Of The Family, Because In The Normal Situation The Husband Manages The House In The Interest Of His Family In The Name Of The Wife. Buys Property That Has No Independent Source Of Income.

Unless Proven, It Is Considered To Be The Husband's Income.

The High Court Said That Unless It Is Proved That A Particular Property Has Been Purchased From The Wife's Income, That Property Is Considered To Have Been Purchased From The Husband's Income. Appellant Saurabh Gupta Had Demanded That He Be Given The Status Of Co-Owner Of One-Fourth Of The Property Purchased By His Father. Her

Plea Was That Since The Property Was Purchased By Her Late Father, She Was A Co-Sharer In It Along With Her Mother.

The Lower Court Had Rejected The Petition

Saurabh Gupta's Mother Is The Defendant In This Suit. Saurabh Gupta Had Filed An Application Seeking A Stay Against Transferring The Property To Any Third Party. Saurabh's Mother Said In A Written Statement That The Property Was Gifted To Her By Her Husband As He Had No Source Of Income. The Application Seeking Interim Injunction Was Rejected By The Lower Court, Against Which Saurabh Gupta Filed An Appeal In The High Court.

Prima Facie Becomes The Property Of A Joint Hindu Family

Accepting The Appeal Of The Appellant, The Court, In Its Judgment Dated February 15, Said That Property Purchased By A Hindu Husband In The Name Of His Housewife Wife Is Considered To Be Purchased From The Personal Income Of The Husband, Since The Wife Has No Income. There Is No Independent Source. The Court Said That Such Property Prima Facie Becomes The Property Of A Joint Hindu Family. In Such Circumstances It Becomes Necessary To Protect That Property From The Creation Of A Third Party.

Neutral Citation No. - 2024: AHC-LKO:13664

Case: - **FIRST APPEAL FROM ORDER No. - 321 Of 2023**

Appellant: - Saurabh Gupta Respondent: - Smt. Archna Gupta And 2 Others

Not Allowing Spouse To Have Sex For A Long Time Is Mental Cruelty: Allahabad High Court

The Above Order Was Given In The Allahabad High Court In A Divorce Related Case. The Husband Had Sought Divorce From His Wife On The Grounds That His Wife Was Not Allowing Him To Have Sexual Relations With Her For A Long Time. Not Living With Him.

The High Court Allowed The Husband To Divorce His Wife On The Grounds Of Cruelty. And Said That On The Part Of The Husband Or Wife, Not Allowing Sexual Relations With One's Spouse For A Long Time Without Sufficient Reason Is Mental Cruelty In Itself.

A Division Bench Of Justice Sunit Kumar And Justice Rajendra Kumar-IV Was Hearing The Case. The Divorce Petition Was Filed In The Family Court On Behalf Of The Husband Under Section 13 Of The Hindu Marriage Act, 1955. The Family Court Had Rejected The Petition. The Husband Approached The High Court Against This.

They Also Get To Know What Arguments The Husband Presented For Divorce.

The Husband Said That Both Of Them Got Married In 1979. After Some Time, The Wife's Behaviour And Conduct Changed. She Refused To Live With Him Like His Wife. Despite Explaining, He Did Not Establish Any

The Husband Had Requested The Court To Reduce The Amount Of Maintenance, Whereas The Wife Claimed To Pay Rs 2 Lakh As Maintenance For Herself And Rs 40,000 To Rs 60,000 Every Month For The Child. The Court Said That The Wife Was Getting A Salary Of Rs 2.5 Lakh Every Month, While The Husband Was Getting $ 7134 Per Month, Which Is Equal To The Wife's Income In Indian Rupees.

The Court Said, 'Although The Husband Is Earning In Dollars, It Cannot Be Ignored That His Expenses Are Also In Dollars.' The Husband Said That His Monthly Expenses Are Around $7000 And He Has Very Little Money Left In The Name Of Savings. The Husband Also Showed Documents In Support Of His Argument.

Noting That Both Would Have To Bear The Responsibility Of Raising The Child, The Court Ruled That The Amount Of Maintenance For The Child Of Rs 40,000 Should Be Reduced To Rs 25,000 Per Month.

Case Title: X V. Y

Disabled Husband Will Not Have To Pay Maintenance: Karnataka High Court

The Karnataka High Court Has Refused To Compel A Man With 75 Per Cent Disability To Pay Maintenance To His Estranged Wife, Overturning A Trial Court Order Seeking His Arrest Or Imposing Fine.

A Single Judge Bench Of Justice M. Nagaprasanna Stressed The Physical Limitations Of The Man And Said, "The Husband Walks With The Help Of Crutches", Making It Impractical To Expect Employment From Him To Pay The Maintenance Expenses.

Due To Marital Discord, The Husband Filed A Petition For Divorce Alleging That The Wife Had Voluntarily Abandoned Him.

Meanwhile, The Wife Sought Interim Maintenance Under Section 24 Of The Hindu Marriage Act, And Was Initially Granted Rs 15,000 Per Month.

Later The Husband Became Disabled And Was Unable To Pay The Maintenance.

The Court Examined The Wife's Employment And The Husband's Disability Certificate And Questioned The Logic Behind Demanding Maintenance From A Disabled Husband.

The Court Expressed Concern About The Financial Pressure On The Husband. The Court Rejected The Wife's Plea For A Higher Amount Of Maintenance And Ordered The Husband's Father To Pay The Amount Outstanding Before The Man Became Disabled.

Priyanka Singh V Pankaj Singh Sengar [WP 48615 Of 2024]

No Right To Maintenance If Separated From Husband Without Valid Reason:

Jharkhand High Court

Jharkhand High Court Has Given A Big Verdict On The Claim Of Maintenance Of The Wife Who Is Separated From Her Husband Without Any Reason. While Hearing A Petition, The Court Said That The Wife Is Living Separately From The Husband Without Any Valid Reason. In Such A Situation, She Cannot Get Money For Maintenance And She Is Not Entitled To It. The Court Also Set Aside The Lower Court Order.

Jharkhand High Court Has Said In Its Order That A Wife Who Lives Separately From Her Husband Without Any Valid Reason Is Not Entitled To Maintenance From The Husband.

While Giving This Decision, The Court Of Justice Subhash Chand Said That In Whatever Evidence Has Been Presented Before The Court In This Case, There Is Nothing That Shows That There Is Any Concrete Reason For The Wife To Separate From Her Husband. In Such A Situation, The Wife Does Not Have The Right To Receive Allowance For Maintenance.

Along With This Direction, The Court Also Cancelled The Order Of The Family Court, In Which The Husband Was Directed To Give Rs 15,000 Every Month To The Wife For Maintenance.

In This Regard, Husband Amit Kachhap Had Filed A Petition In The High Court Challenging The Order Of Ranchi Family Court. The Family Court Had Directed The Husband To Pay Rs 15,000 Every Month To The Wife For Maintenance From October 30, 2017.

What Argument Did The Husband Give Before The Court?

The Court Was Told On Behalf Of The Husband That The Wife Had Left The Husband's House A Few Days After The Marriage. She Started Making Excuses In Some Form Or The Other Every Time.

It Was Told On Behalf Of The Husband That Whatever Allegations The Wife Has Made Against Him Are Not Justified. He Has Left The House Of His Own Free Will.

After This The Wife Applied For Maintenance In The Family Court Of Ranchi. After Hearing This, The Family Court Directed The Husband To Pay Rs 15,000 Every Month For Maintenance.

The High Court Gave Its Verdict After Hearing The Arguments Of Both The Parties.

During The Hearing On Amit Kachhap's Appeal Against This, The High Court Sought Answers From Both The Parties And Directed To Present All The Evidence.

After Looking At All The Evidence, The Court Said That In This Case No Such Evidence Has Been Presented By The Wife, Which Would Show That She Is Upset With Her Husband Or His Family Members Are Harassing Her.

The High Court Said That The Allegations Made By The Wife And The Evidence Provided In Support Of Them Are Full Of Contradictions. The Wife Is Living Separately From Her Husband Without Any Valid Reason.

In Such A Situation, She Cannot Get Money For Maintenance And She Is Not Entitled To It. Along With This, The Court Also Cancelled The Order Of The Lower Court.

Amit Kumar Kachhap Vs. Sangeeta Toppo (Criminal Revision No.512 Of 2023)

Maintenance Obligations Should Not Burden A Husband To The Point Of Marriage Becoming A Punishment: Jharkhand High Court

While Hearing A Case Related To Family Dispute And Alimony, Jharkhand High Court Has Made An Important Comment. The Court Said That It Is The Legal And Moral Responsibility Of The Husband To Maintain The

Wife Who Is Living Separately Due To A Family Dispute, But In The Name Of This, The Husband Should Not Be Burdened In Such A Way That Marriage Becomes A Punishment For Him. Justice Subhash Chand's Court Made This Comment While Hearing A Petition Filed Against An Order Of Dhanbad Family Court. The Family Court Had Ordered To Pay Rs 40 Thousand Per Month As Maintenance Allowance To The Estranged Wife.

Wife's Maintenance Allowance Should Not Be So Much That It Becomes A Burden On The Husband - High Court

After Hearing The Entire Case, The High Court Has Ordered To Reduce This Amount To Rs 25 Thousand Per Month. The Petitioner Has Said In His Petition That He Got Married In The Year 2018. Within A Few Days Of Marriage, His Wife Accused Him Of Dowry And Domestic Violence And Left The House And Started Living With Her Parents. The Wife Had Presented A Claim In The Court For Maintenance Allowance.

While Presenting The Claim, The Wife Had Said That Her Husband Is A Financially Prosperous Businessman And His Total Monthly Income From Various Sources Is Estimated To Be Around Rs 12.5 Lakh. On This, Dhanbad Family Court Directed That The Husband Should Give Maintenance Of Rs 40 Thousand Per Month To His Wife. The High Court Ruled That The Decision Of The Family Court Was Based On Wrong Findings And The Amount Of Maintenance Decided Was Unreasonable.

Case Title: Niraj Kathuria V. State Of Jharkhand

High Court's Order: Divorced Woman To Pay Rs 1 Lakh To Ex-Husband For Misusing Law

Justice Subodh Abhyankar Of The Indore Bench Of The High Court Said, "This Order Of Payment Of Rs 1 Lakh Has Been Issued Only To Warn Unethical Litigants So That They Do Not Throw Dust In The Eyes Of The Courts. Courts Hear Serious Cases And Their

Precious Time Cannot Be Allowed To Be Wasted In Any Way.

The Madhya Pradesh High Court Has Expressed Displeasure Over A Divorced Woman Wasting The Court's Time By Continuing "Immoral Litigation" Against Her Ex-Husband And Elderly In-Laws And Also Imposed A Compensation Of Rs 1 Lakh As A Warning. The Court Found That The Woman, Resident Of Indore, Broke Her Promise Of Divorce By Mutual Consent, Did Not Withdraw The Old Case Against Her Ex-Husband And His Elderly Parents And Misused The Legal Process.

What Did The Court Say?

The Court, While Quashing The Case Registered Against Her On Charges Of Dowry Harassment, Assault And Abortion Without The Woman's Consent, Has Ordered The Divorced Woman To Pay Rs 1 Lakh To Her Ex-Husband.

Justice Subodh Abhyankar Of The Indore Bench Of The High Court Said, "This Order Of Payment Of Rs 1 Lakh Has Been Issued Only To Warn Unethical Litigants So That They Do Not Throw Dust In The Eyes Of The Courts. Courts Hear Serious Cases And Their Precious Time Cannot Be Allowed To Be Wasted In Any Way.

The Single Bench Made This Comment In Its Order While Allowing The Petition Filed By The Woman's Ex-Husband And Her Elderly Parents On March 1. Quoting Records, The Court Said That The Petitioner Man And The Defendant Woman Were Divorced With Mutual Consent On February 2, 2023 And In Lieu Of This, Rs 50 Lakh Has Also Been Given To The Woman By Her Former Husband.

The High Court Said That Despite The Clear Undertaking In The Divorce Deed That Both The Parties Are Committed To Withdraw The Cases Filed Against Each Other, The Divorced Woman Filed The Case Against Her Ex-Husband And His Elderly Parents In 2018. No Effort Was Made To Withdraw The Criminal Case Registered In.

The Case Was Registered Five Years Ago

The Woman Had Registered This Case At Indore's Vijay Nagar Police Station Five Years Ago After Taking Divorce From Her Husband On The Basis Of Mutual Consent. Both Of Them Were Married In The Year 2000 And They Also Have A 20-Year-Old Daughter, Who Is Living With Her Father After Divorce.

MISC. CRIMINAL CASE No. 6308 Of 2022.

Husband Can Seek 'Normal Income Statement' Of Estranged Wife Under RTI To Corroborate Evidence In Maintenance Case: CIC

In A Recent Decision, The Central Information Commission (CIC) Has Mandated The Central Public Information Officer (CPIO) To Provide The Individual With The "General Statement Of Net Taxable Income/Gross Income" Of His Wife For The Specified Time Period In Response To His RTI Application. Gave Instructions.

Information Commissioner Saroj Punhani Relied On Rehmat Bano Vs. Chief Commissioner Of Income Tax, Under Which A Similar Request Made By A Wife For Her Husband Was Allowed By The CIC.

Accordingly, It Ordered,

"...Applying The Same Criteria In Favor Of The Husbands In Pursuance Of The Petition Of The Appellants During The Hearing That Information Is Being Requested To Corroborate The Evidence In The Maintenance Case Pending Against Them, The Commission Directs The CPIO To Provide Only A Compliance Report To This Effect Of The Applicant's Wife For The Specified Time Period Will Be Given To The Applicant Free Of Charge Within 15 Days From The Date Of Receipt Of This Order. Will Be Sent To The Commission By The CPIO Immediately Within 7 Days.

The Appellant (Husband) Filed An RTI Application To Obtain The Income Details (Gross Income/Net Income) Of His Estranged Wife. His Intention Was To Use This Information As Evidence In Court In The Ongoing Maintenance Case Against Him. However, The CPIO Denied The

Information Citing Section 8(1)(J) Of The RTI Act. Dissatisfied With This Decision The Appellant Filed The First Appeal.

The FAA Upheld The CPIO's Response, Saying That Because The Information Relates To Personal Information, Its Disclosure Has No Connection To Any Public Activity Or Interest. Feeling Aggrieved And Dissatisfied The Appellant Immediately Approached The Commission With A Second Appeal.

The CIC Pointed Out That The Delhi High Court In Vijay Prakash Vs. Union Of India Had Observed That In Private Disputes Such As The Present Dispute Between Husband And Wife "…The Basic Protection Is Provided On The Basis Of Exemption (From Disclosure). Therefore, Section 8(1)(J) Of The Act Cannot Be Removed Or Disturbed.

The CIC Then Referred To The Decision Of The Commission's Coordination Bench In The Rehmat Bano Case, Wherein Disclosure Of Gross Income To An Estranged Wife Has Been Permitted On Grounds Of Maintenance Of The Family And Livelihood.

CIC Further Said That The Said Decision In Sunita Jain Vs. Pawan Kumar Jain And Others (W.A. No. 168/2015) And Madhya Pradesh High Court In Sunita Jain Vs. Bharat Sanchar Nigam Limited And Others (W.A. No. 170/2015) And Also By The Bombay High Court In Rajesh Ramchandra Kidile Vs. Maharashtra SIC And Others (W.P. No. 1766 Of 2016) (Nagpur Bench). It Is Based On Two High Court Decisions In The Case Of.

Both The Courts, While Evaluating Section 8(1)(J) Of The RTI Act, Emphasized That A Partner Should Have The Right To Know The Remuneration Of The Other Partner. Such Information Can No Longer Be Classified As 'Purely Personal'.

File No: CIC/CCITD/A/2023/622483

Wife Living In Adultery Not Entitled To Maintenance From Husband Under Domestic Violence Act: Karnataka High Court

While Considering The Instant Petition Wherein A Wife Had Challenged The Order Of The Sessions Judge Whereby Which He Had Set Aside The

Order Of Granting Maintenance To The Petitioner Under Section 12 Of The Protection Of Women From Domestic Violence Act, 2005 Along With Compensation; The Bench Of Rajendra Badamikar, J., Dismissed The Petition Stating That When The Wife Is Staying In Adultery, The Question Of Claim Of Maintenance Does Not Arise At All. The Contention That The Petitioner Is A Legally Wedded Wife And Entitled For Maintenance Cannot Be Accepted In View Of Her Conduct, Who Is Not Honest And Is Leading Adulterous Life. The Petitioner Had Filed The Petition Under Section 12 Of The D.V. Act Claiming Protection Order Under Section 18, Residential Order Under Section 19 And Monetary Benefit Under Section 20 In The Form Of Maintenance Of Rs.3,000/- Per Month And Compensation Of Rs.25,000/- Under Section 22. After Appreciating The Oral And Documentary Evidence, The Magistrate Granted A Protection Order Under Section 18 Of The D.V. Act And He Also Awarded Maintenance Of Rs.1,500/- To The Petitioner With Rs.1,000/- Towards Rent Allowance And Also Awarded Rs.5,000/- Towards Compensation. The Afore-Stated Order Was Challenged By The Husband And The Sessions Judge After Re-Appreciating The Evidence, Set Aside The Order Of The Magistrate. The Aggrieved Wife Thus Filed The Instant Revision Petition. Counsel For The

Petitioner Argued That The Revision Petition Should Be Allowed As The Petitioner Is A Legally Wedded Wife Of Respondent And It Is The Duty Of Husband To Maintain His Wife. It Was Asserted That Since The Husband Is Having An Illicit Relationship With His Relative, Domestic Violence Is Required To Be Inferred. Per Contra, Counsel For The Husband Argued That The Marriage Was Dissolved By The Competent Court By Granting A Decree On The Ground Of Adultery As Well As Cruelty. He Also Contended That Evidence Disclosed That The Petitioner Had Eloped With Neighbour And All Along, She Refused To Stay With Her Husband And Showed Her Interest To Stay With Her Paramour. It Was Further Contended That Though Petitioner Is Legally Wedded Wife, Looking To Her Conduct Having Illicit Relationship, She Is Not Entitled For Any Maintenance. Perusing The Facts And Arguments Presented In The Matter, The Court Noted That It Is The Specific Contention Of The Respondent Husband Is That The Petitioner Has Eloped With A Neighbour. The Court Also Noted That The Couple Are Now Divorced And Same Has Not Been Challenged By The Wife. The Court Also Took Note Of The Oral And Documentary Evidence And Pointed Out That It Clearly Establishes That The Petitioner Is Not Honest Towards Her Husband. The Court Opined That Since The Petitioner Is Claiming Maintenance, She Must Prove That She Is Honest And When She Herself Is Not Honest, She Cannot Pin-Point Her Fingers Towards Her Husband. The Court Also Pointed Out That The Magistrate Had Failed To Appreciate The Aspects Of The Case And In A Mechanical Way, Awarded The Maintenance And Compensation, Which Is A Perverse Order. The Sessions Judge On The Other Hand Has Re-Appreciated The Oral And Documentary Evidence And Has Rightly Rejected The Claim Of The Petitioner In View Of The Fact That She Was Leading An Adulterous Life….

Impact Of The Decision The Karnataka High Court's Decision Has Significant Implications For Cases Involving Adultery And Maintenance Claims. It Establishes A Precedent That A Wife Engaged In An Extramarital Affair May Forfeit Her Right To Claim Maintenance From Her Husband. This Precedent Underscores The Importance Of Honesty And Credibility When Seeking Maintenance Through Legal Avenues.

Conclusion The Karnataka High Court's Judgment In The Case Of An Adulterous Wife's Right To Claim Maintenance Provides Valuable Insights Into The Complex Legal Landscape Of Family Law In India. The Decision Underscores The Importance Of Honesty And Credibility When Seeking Maintenance And Ensures That Individuals Engaged In Extramarital Affairs Do Not Exploit Legal Provisions Meant To Protect The Genuinely Aggrieved. In Essence, The Court's Ruling Establishes A Crucial Precedent, Emphasizing That A Wife Involved In An Adulterous Relationship May Not Have The Legal Standing To Claim Maintenance From Her Husband. It Highlights The Need For Clean Hands When Pursuing Legal Remedies In Such Cases. While This Judgment Clarifies The Legal Position On Adultery And Maintenance Claims, It Also Raises Questions About The Broader Implications Of Personal Conduct On Legal Rights Within The Realm Of Family Law. As Society Continues To Evolve, The Intersection Of Morality And Legality In Family Disputes Remains A Subject Of Ongoing Debate And Legal Interpretation.

NC: 2023: KHC:33789

CRL.RP No. 56 Of 2016

Disgruntled Wives Are Using IPC Section 498A As A Weapon Instead Of A Shield:

Jharkhand High Court

The Judge Made These Observations While Quashing Criminal Proceedings Initiated By A Woman Who Alleged That Her Sister-In-Law And Brother-In-Law Had Committed Torturous Acts Against Her.

The High Court Of Jharkhand Quashed Proceedings Against Petitioners Accused Under Section 498A Of The IPC And Held That The Role Played By These Petitioners Is Not Disclosed And There Are Only General And Omnibus Allegations Against The Petitioners And The Present Complaint Case Failed To Establish Specific Allegations Against These Petitioners And Further 498A Is Being Used As Weapon Rather Than Shield By Disgruntled Wives.

Brief Facts:

The Present Petition Was Filed For Quashing Of Entire Criminal Proceedings Against The Petitioners After A Complaint Was Filed After A Case Was Filed Against Him Under Section 498A After The Complainant Alleged That She Was Tortured By The Petitioners.

Contentions Of The Petitioner:

The Learned Counsel Appearing On Behalf Of The Petitioners Contended That Only General And Omnibus Allegations Against The Petitioners And Further Submitted That On 01.04.2013, Petitioner No.2 Was Travelling And The Allegations Are Made That On 02.04.2013 Torture Was Made By These Petitioners, Which Falsify The Case Against The Petitioners Who Happened To Be Brother-In-Law And Sister-In-Law Of The Complainant Respectively.

Observations Of The Court:

The Court Referred To The Facts Of The Case And Observed That The Petitioners Were Residing In Hyderabad, Whereas, The Alleged Place Of Occurrence Is At Dhanbad And Further It Was Alleged In The Complaint Petition That On 02.04.2013, The Accused Came To Dhanbad And Was Tortured The Complainant But The Document Issued By The South-Central Railway Clearly Suggested That False Statement Had Been Made In The Complaint Petition.

Further The Court Stated That Section 498-A Of The Indian Penal Code Was Inserted In The Statute With The Laudable Object Of Punishing Cruelty At The Hands Of Husband Or His Relatives But There Is A Phenomenal Increase In Matrimonial Disputes In Recent Years And It Appears That In Many Cases, The Object Of Section 498-A Of The Indian Penal Code Is Being Misused And The Said Section Is Used As Weapon Rather Than Shield By Disgruntled Wives. It Was Stated That Such Type Of Cases Are Being Filed In The Heat Of The Moment Over Trivial Issues Without Proper Deliberations An Further Relied On The Judgment In Preeti Gupta Vs State Of Jharkhand In Furtherance Of Same And Further Stated That Little Matrimonial Skirmishes Suddenly Erupt Which Often Assume Serious Proportions Resulting In Commission Of Heinous Crimes In Which Elders Of The Family Are Falsely Implicated By The Wives And The Court Should Be Careful In Proceeding Against The Distant Relatives In Crimes Pertaining To Matrimonial Disputes And Dowry Deaths.

The Court Stated That In The Present Case, The Role Played By These Petitioners Is Not Disclosed And There Are Only General And Omnibus Allegations Against The Petitioners And The Present Complaint Case Failed To Establish Specific Allegation Against These Petitioners.

The Decision Of The Court: The Court Allowed The Petition And Quashed The Entire Criminal Proceedings Against The Petitioners.

Case No.: Cr.M.P. No. 2579 Of 2013.

Wife Does Not Have The Right To Get Maintenance From Her Husband If She Willingly Leaves The Matrimonial Home: Allahabad High Court

The Allahabad High Court Has Declined To Grant Maintenance To A Woman Who Voluntarily Left The Matrimonial Home.

Justice Prashant Kumar's Bench, While Hearing The Case, Said That It Is Clear From The Provision Of Section 125 (4) Of Crpc That If A Wife Refuses To Live With Her Husband, She Has No Right To Get Maintenance From Her Husband, And Will Not Have Rights.

The Court Quashed The Order Of The Mathura Family Court.

The Woman Claimed That She Had Not Left The Matrimonial Home Of Her Own Free Will. She Had Said That Her In-Laws Used To Demand More Dowry Than Her.

It Was Said In The Petition That The Petitioner And His Wife Were Married In 2015. After The Marriage In 2017, The Medical Examination Of The Woman Revealed That She Could Not Become A Mother, Following Which The Petitioner Lodged A Complaint With The Police Against His Wife And Her Family Members. It Was Alleged By The Petitioner That His Wife And Her Family Members Had Assaulted Him And His Family Members.

The Petitioner Had Applied For Divorce In January 2018.

In February 2018, The Woman Filed A Case Against Her Husband And His Family Members Under Sections 498A, 504, 323, 377 Of The IPC Under The Dowry Prohibition Act. The Counsel For The Woman Argued That She Had Not Left Her Matrimonial Home. No Woman Leaves Her Matrimonial Home Without Any Reason. She Was Forced To Do So By Her In-Laws.

Case: Gaurav Vashishtha V State Of U.P. And Another

(CRIMINAL REVISION No. – 4498 Of 2022)

Magistrate Cannot Impose More Than 12 Months Sentence For Non-Payment Of Maintenance: Bombay HC

The Bombay High Court, In A Recent Landmark Judgment, Has Established Crucial Sentencing Limits For Magistrates In Cases Of Non-Payment Of Maintenance. The Case, Vikram Ramesh Rughani Vs The State Of Maharashtra & Anr, Writ Petition (ST) No. 2435 Of 2024, Sets A Clear Precedent. This Article Provides An In-Depth Analysis Of The Judgment. While Clearly Drawing The Red Lines For The Maximum Sentence That A Magistrate Can Impose For Non-Payment Of Maintenance, We See That The Bombay High Court In A Most Learned, Laudable, Landmark And Latest Judgment Titled Vikram Ramesh Rughani Vs The State Of Maharashtra & Anr In Writ Petition (ST) No. 2435 Of 2024 And Cited In Neutral Citation: 2024:BHC-AS:8917 That Was Reserved On February 22, 2024 And Then Finally Pronounced On February 26, 2024 Has Minced Just No Words To Hold In No Uncertain Terms That A Magistrate Cannot Impose More Than 12 Months Sentence For Non-Payment Of Maintenance In An Application Under Section 125(3) Crpc. We Need To Note Here That A Magistrate Had Sentenced A Husband To Undergo Simple Imprisonment Of 47 Months For Default In Payment Of Maintenance To The Wife Of 47 Months . In This Context, It Must Be Mentioned That The Magistrate In Pursuance Of This Order Had Issued An Arrest Warrant Against The Husband Under Section 125(3) Of Crpc Read With Section 28 Of The Protection Of Women From Domestic Violence Act, 2005 (D.V. Act) For Recovery Of Interim Maintenance After No Payments Were Made. The High Court Was Thus Required To Consider The Moot Question As To Whether The Power Of The Magistrate To Sentence A Defaulter For Non-Payment Of Maintenance Granted Under The D.V. Proceedings Was Restricted To Impose Imprisonment For A Period Of 12 Months Under Sub-Section (3) Of Section 125 Of Crpc. We Definitely Need To Note That The Single Judge Bench Comprising Of Hon'ble Ms Justice Sharmila U Deshmukh Explicitly Stated That, "Plain Reading Of The Proviso Makes It Evident That The Proviso Creates An Embargo On Power Of

Magistrate To Issue Warrant For Recovery Of Amount Which Has Become Due Beyond Period Of One Year…The Proviso When Read With The Main Section Makes It Evident That By Limiting The Application For Issuance Of Warrant To A Period Of 12 Months, The Power Of The Magistrate Stands Restricted To Impose Maximum Punishment Of Imprisonment For Period 12 Months." We Thus See That The Bombay High Court Sets Aside The Order Of The Magistrate In This Leading Case Providing Relief To The Petitioner And The Petition Thus Succeeded. Very Rightly So!

At The Very Outset, This Brief, Brilliant, Bold And Balanced Judgment Authored By The Single Judge Bench Comprising Of Hon'ble Ms Justice Sharmila U Deshmukh Sets The Ball In Motion By First And Foremost Putting Forth In Para 1 That, "Rule. Learned AGP Waives Notice On Behalf Of State. Mr. Bhuvan Singh Waives Notice On Behalf Of Respondent No2. With Consent Of Parties, The Petition Is Taken Up Forthwith For Final Hearing." While Stating The Purpose Of The Petition, The Bench Discloses In Para 2 That, "By This Petition Challenge Is To The Order Dated 20th January, 2024 Passed By The Metropolitan Magistrate In C.C. No 96/DV/2018 Sentencing The Petitioner To Undergo Simple Imprisonment Of 47 Months For Default In Payment Of Maintenance Of 47 Months With The Condition That If The Petitioner Paid The Amount Earlier, He Shall Be Released Forthwith."

To Put Things In Perspective, The Bench While Elaborating On Facts Of Case Envisages In Para 3 That, "The Facts Of The Case Are That C.C. No. 96/DV/2018 Was Preferred By The Respondent No 2 Wife Under The Provisions Of Protection Of Women From Domestic Violence Act, 2005 (D.V. Act) On 18th August, 2018 Seeking Various Reliefs Under Section 18, 19, 20, 21, And 22 Of The D.V. Act. By Order Dated 23rd September, 2019, Passed Under Section 23 Of The D.V. Act, The Metropolitan Magistrate Interalia Directed The Petitioner To Pay Sum Of Rs. 15,000/- Per Month As Interim Maintenance To The Applicant And A Sum Of Rs. 10,000/- Per Month To Their Daughter Mahek. By An Application Dated 6th January, 2020 Filed Under Section 25 Of The D.V. Act, The Petitioner Sought Modification Of The Interim Maintenance Order, Which Is Stated To Be Pending. As The Interim Maintenance Was Being Paid Intermittently In Instalments, An Application For Issuance Of Arrest Warrant Came To Be Filed By Respondent No. 1-Wife On 27th July, 2023 Setting Out Details

Of The Part Payments Made On Various Dates From 4th December, 2019 To 10th July, 2023 Amounting To Rs. 3,25,000/-. It Was Contended That The Arrears Of Maintenance Of 59 Months Aggregates To Rs. 11,50,000/- As From The Date Of Filing Of The Application The Maintenance Has Been Granted Out Of Which Only A Sum Of Rs. 3,25,000/- Has Been Received. By Order Dated 8th November, 2023, The Metropolitan Magistrate Observed That No Payments Were Made After 10rd July, 2023 And Issued Arrest Warrant Against The Petitioner Under Section 125 (3) Of Cr.P.C. Read With Section 28 Of The D.V. Act For Recovery Of Interim Maintenance Of Rs. 11,58,000/-. Subsequently, An Application Was Filed On 16th December, 2023 By The Respondent No 2 Wife For Reissuing Of Arrest Warrant. On The Same Date Another Application Was Filed By The Respondent No 2 Wife Seeking Issuance Of Arrest Warrant Now Contending That The Arrears Of Maintenance Is For 64 Months Amounting To Rs 16,00,000/ Out Of Which Only Rs 3,25,000/ Has Been Paid. On The Application Seeking Re-Issuance Of Arrest Warrant, Arrest Warrant Was Issued On 27th December, 2023. The Arrest Warrant Came To Be Executed And The Petitioner Was Produced Before The Metropolitan Magistrate And By Order Dated 20th January, 2024, The Metropolitan Magistrate Noted That The Petitioner Is Willing To Deposit Rs 1,00,000/ And He Be Permitted To Deposit. It Was Held That Despite Deposit Of Rs 1,00,000/ There Are Arrears Of Rs 11,75,000/. Resultantly, The Petitioner Was Sentenced To Simple Imprisonment For The Period Of 47 Months For The Default In Payment Of Arrears Of Maintenance Of 47 Months." As We See, The Bench Points Out In Para 8 That, "The Issue Which Arises For Consideration In The Present Case Is Whether The Power Of The Magistrate To Sentence A Defaulter For Non-Payment Of Maintenance Granted Under The D.V. Proceedings Is Restricted To Impose Imprisonment For Period Of 12 Months By Virtue Of The Proviso To Sub Section (3) Of Section 125 Of Cr.P.C. In The Instant Case, The Petitioner Has Been Sentenced To Imprisonment For A Period Of 47 Months For Default In Payment Of Maintenance Of 47 Months."

Do Note, The Bench Notes In Para 11 That, "In Exercise Of Powers Conferred By Section 37 Of The D.V. Act, The Central Government Has Framed Rules In The Year 2006. Sub Rule (5) Of Rule 6 Of The Rules Of 2006 Provides That The Application Under Section 12 Shall Be Dealt With

And The Orders Enforced In The Same Manner Laid Down Under Section 125 Of The Cr.P.C. If That Be The Position In Law, While Exercising The Power Under Section 125(3) For Enforcing The Orders Of Maintenance, The Provisions Of Cr.P.C Governs The Proceedings."

Be It Noted, The Bench Notes In Para 13 That, "Sub Section 3 Of Section 125 Of Cr.P.C. Empowers The Magistrate For Every Breach Of The Order To Issue Warrant For Levying The Amount Due And For Sentencing The Person For The Whole Or Any Part Of Each Month's Maintenance Remaining Unpaid To Imprisonment For A Term Which May Extend To One Month Or Until Payment If Sooner Made. Proviso To Sub Section (3) Of Section 125 Restricts The Power Of The Magistrate To Issue Warrant For Recovery Of The Amount Due Unless Application Is Made To The Court To Levy Such Amount Within A Period Of One Year From The Date On Which It Becomes Due. Upon Holistic Reading Of Sub Section 3 Of Section 125, It Is Evident That The Same Provides For Maximum Imprisonment Of One Month For Each Month's Maintenance Or Any Part Thereof Remaining Unpaid, Which Application For Issuance Of Warrant Is Required To Be Filed Within A Period Of One Year From The Date It Becomes Due." Most Significantly, The Bench Minces Absolutely No Words To Mandate In Para 14 That, "There Has Been Considerable Debate On The Proviso To Sub Section (3) As To Whether The Proviso Limits The Power Of The Magistrate To Sentence The Defaulter To A Term Exceeding 12 Months. Plain Reading Of The Proviso Makes It Evident That The Proviso Creates An Embargo On Power Of Magistrate To Issue Warrant For Recovery Of Amount Which Has Become Due Beyond Period Of One Year. Although On First Blush It Appears That The Proviso Deals With The Limitation For Filing Of Application And Bars Issuance Of Warrant In Respect Of Any Amount Unless An Application Is Made Within Period Of One Year From The Date From Which The Amount Has Become Due, The Proviso When Read With The Main Section Makes It Evident That By Limiting The Application For Issuance Of Warrant To A Period Of 12 Months, The Power Of The Magistrate Stands Restricted To Impose Maximum Punishment Of Imprisonment For Period 12 Months. If An Application Cannot Be Filed Seeking Warrant For Recovery Of Amount Remaining Unpaid For Period Of More Than One Year, There Is No Question Of Imprisonment Being Imposed For A Term Exceeding One Year. The Period Of 12 Months Is The Outer Limit." Equally Significant Is What Is Then Postulated In Para 15 That, "In This Context, It

Will Be Profitable To Refer To Section 29 Of Cr.P.C Which Provides That The Court Of Magistrate Of First Class May Pass A Sentence Of Imprisonment For A Term Not Exceeding Three Years And/Or Fine. Reading The Provisions Of Section 125(3) With Section 29 Of Cr.P.C And Section 28 Of D.V. Act, I Am Not Inclined To Accept The Submission Of Learned Counsel For Respondent No. 2 Wife That As The D.V Proceedings Provide For Civil Remedies, There Is No Restriction On Sentencing Powers Of Metropolitan Magistrate."

No Less Significant Is That It Is Held In Para 24 That, "Having Regard To The Discussion Above, Petition Succeeds And The Impugned Order Dated 20th January, 2024 Is Quashed And Set Aside. Consequently, The Petitioner Is Directed To Be Released Forthwith. It Is Clarified That The Quashing Of The Impugned Order Does Not Restrict The Respondent No. 2 Wife From Filing Fresh Application For Issuance Of Warrant For Non-Payment Of Maintenance Setting Out The Relevant Details. It Is Open For The Respondent No. 2 Wife To File Separate Applications For Issuance Of Warrant Subject To Outer Limit Of 12 Defaults Being Clubbed In One Application. If Such Application Is Filed, The Metropolitan Magistrate To Consider The Same In Accordance With The Observations Made Herein. Rule Is Made Absolute." All Told, We Thus See That The Bombay High Court Has Made It Indubitably Clear That A Magistrate Cannot Impose More Than 12 Months Sentence For The Non-Payment Of Maintenance In An Application Under Section 125(3) Of The Crpc. We Thus See Here That The Petition Of The Petitioner Succeeds. The Petitioner Is Thus Directed To Be Released By The Bombay High Court. Very Rightly So! Conclusion: In Conclusion, The Bombay High Court's Judgment Firmly Establishes That A Magistrate Cannot Impose More Than A 12-Month Sentence For Non-Payment Of Maintenance Under Section 125(3) Of The Crpc. The Petitioner's Success Underscores The Importance Of Adhering To Statutory Limits In Such Cases, Ensuring A Balanced Approach To Justice. The Court's Clear Articulation Of Restrictions On Sentencing Powers Provides A Significant Precedent For Future Cases In Similar Contexts.

WRIT PETITION (ST) NO.2435 OF 2024

Muslim Wife Initiating Divorce Not Entitled To Maintenance From Husband U/S 125 Crpc From Date Of 'Khula': Kerala High Court

In A Revolutionary Ruling, The Kerala High Court Reiterated That A Muslim Woman Who Obtains A Divorce Through 'Khula' Isn't Permitted To Request Maintenance From Her Husband Once The Divorce Becomes Official. The Understanding Of Islamic Divorce Practices And Their Legal Ramifications Is Expected To Undergo A Substantial Change As A Consequence Of This Verdict.

Understanding 'Khula'

The Muslim Community Follows The "Khula" Divorce Method, Which Is Requested And Accepted/Consented By The Wife. It Often Involves The Wife Providing Consideration To Her Husband For Her Release From The Marital Bond. This Practice, Which Has Long Been Accepted In Islamic Law, Grants Women A Voice In Ending A Marriage.

The Legal Interpretation

Muslim Women May Request Support Under Section 125 Of The Code Of Criminal Procedure (Crpc) Until They Remarry, According To Justice A. Badharudeen. However, According To Section 125(4) Of The Crpc, A Wife Is Not Entitled To Financial Assistance If She Chooses To Live Apart From Her Husband Or If They Do So With Mutual Consent.

The Court Stated That A Wife's Decision To Choose "Khula" To End The Marriage Is Analogous To Her Decision To Not Reside With Her Husband As Outlined In Section 125(4) Of The Crpc. Consequently, As Of "Khula," She Won't Be Entitled To Financial Maintenance.

The Ruling Came From A Case Where A Man Appealed A Family Court Judgment Ordering Him To Provide His Ex-Wife And Kid A Monthly Stipend. The Court Noted That The Parties Had Been Living Separately Since December 31, 2018, And The Legal Battle Began In 2019. The Woman, Who Was Also Unemployed, Sought Financial Assistance, Claiming Their Separation Due To The Husband's Alleged Abuse And Extramarital Affairs. The Court, However, Made Clear That Maintenance Must Be Paid Up Until The 'Khula' Divorce Is Formally Executed, After Which The Obligation Ceases.

Significance Of The Verdict

This Ruling Defines The 'Khula' Divorces' Legal Position With Regard To Maintenance And Is A Crucial Development Because It Emphasizes How Significant It Is For Both Parties To Agree And Have A Thorough Grasp Of The Implications Associated With These Divorce Proceedings. The Court Also Emphasized How Divorced Muslim Women Are Protected Financially Under Islamic Law, Based On Multiple Supreme Court Rulings, Until They Find New Husbands Or Adequate Assistance Is Provided Until Then.

The Kerala High Court's Judgment Establishes The 'Khula' Divorce's Legal Status And Its Implications On Assistance. It Preserves The Idea That "Khula" Is A Voluntary Action Similar To Declining To Cohabitate. Hence, No Maintenance Is Owed As Of The "Khula" Date. This Decision Marks A Significant Turning Point In The Continuing Evolution Of Islamic Divorce Jurisprudence In India.

Major Arguments On The Changing Legal Environment Pertaining To Muslim Women's Rights And Entitlements During Divorce Have Been Brought Up By The Kerala High Court's Decision. It Also Highlights How Essential It Is To Accept Individual Choices Made In A Religious Setting While Abiding By The Law. The 'Khula' Divorce And The Determination Of Maintenance Rights Now Stand On A Foundation Because Of This Significant Ruling, Ushering In A New Era In Indian Law Concerning Islamic Divorce.

R.P(F.C).No.98 Of 2020

Day-To-Day Bickering Between Husband & Wife Not 'Cruelty' Under Section 498A IPC:

Calcutta High Court

Single-Judge Justice Sugato Majumdar, Therefore, Quashed The Conviction Under Section 498A Of IPC Of A Man Who Was Charged For Subjecting His Wife To Mental And Physical Cruelty.

It, However, Upheld His Conviction And Sentence Of ₹1,000 Fine Under Section 323 Of The IPC.

"Cruelty Contemplated In Section 498A Of The Indian Penal Code Is Different From Day To Day Bickering Between The Husband And Wife. Sweeping And General Allegations Cannot Be Relied Upon To Conclude That Offence Under Section 498A Has Been Perpetrated," The Court Held.

The Trial Court Committed An Error In Coming To Conclusion That The Appellant Husband Is Guilty Of Offence Under Section 498A, The Court Further Concluded.

"There Are Latches On The Part Of The Trial Court In Appreciation Of Evidence. Therefore, Conviction Under Section 498-A Is Liable To Be Quashed," The Bench Held.

Ranjan Das Vs State Of West Bengal

A Bench Led By Justice Vikram Nath Deprecates The Conduct Of The Rajasthan Police Officer And Her Father For Misusing State Machinery To File False Dowry Demand Cases Against Her Husband

The Supreme Court Has Ordered The Father Of A Woman Police Officer In Rajasthan To Shell Out Rs 5 Lakh For Lodging False Dowry Demand Cases Under Section 498A Of The IPC At Different Places Against Her Husband To Harass Him.

"We Thus Deprecate This Practice Of State Machinery Being Misused For Ulterior Motives And For Causing Harassment To The Other Side, We Are Thus Inclined To Impose Cost On The Respondent No. 2 (Woman's Father) In Order To Compensate The Appellant," A Bench Of Justice Vikram Nath And Justice Prashant Kumar Mishra Said In Its April 19 Verdict.

"Without Going Into These Statutory Provisions And The Case Laws Relied Upon By The Parties, We Are Convinced That The Impugned Proceedings Are Nothing But An Abuse Of The Process Of Law," The Bench Said, Allowing The Husband's Appeal Against The Rajasthan High

Court's March 6, 2017 Order Dismissing His Petition Seeking Quashing Of An FIR Lodged At Women Police Station, Udaipur Under Sections 498A, 406, 384, 420 And 120(B) Of Indian Penal Code.

Imposing Costs Of Rs 5 Lakh On The Woman Police Officer's Father, The Top Court Directed Him To Deposit The Amount With The Supreme Court's Registrar In Four Weeks. It Ordered That 50% Of The Amount May Be Transmitted In The Account Of The Supreme Court Legal Services Committee And The Remaining 50% To The Appellant Husband.

The Appellant/Husband — A Hisar-Based Chartered Accountant -- And The Respondent No. 3 Wife (Deputy Superintendent Of Police, Udaipur, At The Time Of Marriage) Came In Contact In June 2014 Through The Internet. They Got Engaged On February 18, 2015 And The Marriage Was Solemnised At Udaipur On March 21, 2015.

The Woman's Father Filed A Complaint At The Hisar Police Station For Alleged Dowry Demand Under Section 498A Of The IPC Against The Appellant And His Family Members On October 10, 2015. After Five Days, Another Complaint Was Registered At Udaipur By The Woman's Father Against The Appellant Husband On The Same Set Of Allegations Under Section 498A Of The IPC And Certain Other Provisions Of Law Alleging That The Appellant Subjected His Wife To Cruelty.

While The Hisar Court Acquitted The Accused Husband On August 2, 2017, The Rajasthan High Court Refused To Quash The FIR Registered At Udaipur, Forcing Him To Move The Top Court.

"In The Facts And Circumstances As Recorded Above, We Are Of The View That Respondent Nos. 2 (Woman's Father) And 3 (Woman Police Officer) Had Been Misusing Their Official Position By Lodging Complaints One After The Other. Further, Their Conduct Of Neither Appearing

Before The Trial Court At Hisar Nor Withdrawing Their Complaint At Hisar Would Show That Their Only Intention Was To Harass The Appellant By First Making Him Face A Trial At Hisar And Then Again At Udaipur," The Bench Noted.

"'The Respondent No. 3 (Wife) Was A Gazetted Police Officer At The Relevant Time And Was Also Well Aware Of The Laws, In Particular The Crpc And The Provisions Thereto. Neither The Complainant (Her Father) Nor The Victim (Wife) Entered The Witness Box Before The Hisar Court Allowing Total Wastage Of The Valuable Time Of The Court And The Investigating Agency. Merely Because She Was A Police Officer, She First Managed To Get An FIR Lodged At Hisar Through Her Father, And Thereafter She Moved To Her Hometown At Udaipur And Got Another Complaint Lodged By Her Father Within A Week," The Top Court Said, Deprecating The Conduct Of The Police Officer And Her Father.

"It Is Not Denied By The Respondent Nos. 2 And 3 That They Did Not Lodge A Complaint At Hisar. They Also Did Not File An Application Withdrawing Their Complaint On The Grounds That It Was Wrongly Filed Here Or That The Said Complaint May Be Transferred To Udaipur For Investigation As The Offence Was Committed At Udaipur. They Allowed The Investigating Agency To Continue To Investigate In Which Their Statements Were Also Recorded,"

CRIMINAL APPEAL NO. OF 2024

(Special Leave To Petition (Crl.) No.2520 OF 2017)

Parteek Bansal Vs State Of Rajasthan And Ors

Prolonged Separation From Spouse Without Cause Itself Cruelty U/S 13(1)(Ia)

Hindu Marriage Act: Allahabad High Court

The High Court Has Upheld The Divorce Granted By The Court Below To A Couple Living Separately For Almost 13 Years.

In The Divorce Petition Filed By The Husband, The Court Below Had Decided The Issue Of Dissertation Against Him. However, Divorce Was Granted On Grounds Of Mental Cruelty Inflicted By The Wife On The Husband.

The Bench Held That Cruelty Need Not Only Be Physical In Nature. In Case Of Mental Cruelty, It May Be Impossible For The Spouse To Continue In The Martial Relationship.

Since The Wife Had Admitted That They Had Not Lived Together Continuously, The Court Held

"We, Therefore, Find That Apart From Issue No. 2 Of Cruelty The Court Below Appreciated That It Is A Case Of Irretrievable Breakdown Even If The Desertion Is Not Proved As Per Definition Of Section 13 (1)(Ia) And (Ib). Admittedly At Least 13 Years Have Passed Since Both Are Living Separately, Which By Itself Amounts To Cruelty Under Section 13 (1)(Ia) Of The Act."

Factual Background

As Per Factual Matrix Of The Case, Marriage Between The Parties Was Solemnized As Per Hindu Rites In 2002 And The Wife Lived At Her Paternal Home After Marriage For Some Time. She Went To Live With

Her Husband For A Brief Period, Thereafter, Went Back To Her Paternal Home And Then Joined Service In A Different City From Her Husband. Though Initially The Wife Moved With Her Husband To Mumbai, She Eventually Moved Away.

In The Divorce Petition, The Husband Asserted That He Was Subjected To Mental And Physical Cruelty. He Asserted That He Was Deserted By His Wife And There Was Irretrievable Breakdown Of Marriage. However, In The Written Statement, The Wife Had Alleged Beating And Torture And Demand Of Dowry. She Had Further Alleged Adultery.

During The Divorce Proceedings, Conciliation Was Tried, However, Since The Wife Had Not Appeared On The Subsequent Date, It Was Deemed That She Was Not Interested In Conciliation And The Court Below Proceeded With Recording Evidence. The Court Below Held The Marriage Had Irretrievably Breakdown Even If The Desertion Is Not Proved As Per Definition Of Section 13 (1)(Ia) (Cruelty) And (Ib) (Dissertation).

The Court Also Held That Since The Wife Was Unable To Prove The Allegations Of Extra Marital Affair Against The Husband. The Court Also Noted That The Allegations Regarding Physical Torture Made By The Wife Were False Since No FIR Was Lodged And Her Eye Problem Had Been Persisting Since Before The Marriage. Accordingly, The Court Below Held That Mental Cruelty Was Caused To The Husband.

High Court Verdict

The Court Observed That Living Separately For More Than 13 Years Itself Amounts To Cruelty Under Section 13(1)(Ia).

The Court Relied On Rakesh Raman Vs. Smt. Kavita Wherein Relying On A Judgment Of Its Three-Judge Bench In Samar Ghosh Vs. Jaya Ghosh, The Supreme Court Observed That Mental Cruelty Includes

"Where There Has Been A Long Period Of Continuous Separation, It May Fairly Be Concluded That The Matrimonial Bond Is Beyond Repair. The

Marriage Becomes A Fiction Though Supported By A Legal Tie. By Refusing To Sever That Tie, The Law In Such Cases, Does Not Serve The Sanctity Of Marriage; On The Contrary, It Shows Scant Regard For The Feelings And Emotions Of The Parties. In Such Like Situations, It May Lead To Mental Cruelty."

Further, Reliance Was Placed On Rajib Kumar Roy Vs. Sushmita Saha Wherein The Supreme Court Held That

"Whatever May Be The Justification For The Two Living Separately, With So Much Of Time Gone By, Any Marital Love Or Affection, Which May Have Been Between The Parties, Seems To Have Dried Up. This Is A Classic Case Of Irretrievable Breakdown Of Marriage".

Relying On The Decision Of The Supreme Court In Samar Ghosh, The Court Held That Since Undue Harassment And Mental Cruelty Had Been Established Before The Court Below, The Divorce Was Rightly Granted.

Neutral Citation No. - 2024:AHC:4946-DB

Case :- FIRST APPEAL No. - 177 Of 2017

Wife Attempts Suicide; HC Allows Man's Divorce Plea, Citing Wife's Mental Cruelty

Chhattisgarh High Court Has Held That Wife Attempting To Commit Suicide; Assaulting Her Mother-In-Law, Son Of Her Jeth (Brother-In-Law); Pressing Neck Of Her Daughter & Husband; Obtaining Treatment From A Psychiatrist; And Jumped To The Neighbour's House From The Roof Of Her Marital House Amounts To Causing Mental Cruelty. Husband Entitled For A Decree Of Divorce

The Division Bench Of Prashant Kumar Mishra And N.K. Chandravanshi, JJ., While Finding Error In Trial Court's Decision Held That Wife Attempting To Commit Suicide And Consistently Showing Abnormality In Her Behaviour By Pressing Neck Of Daughter And Husband, Jumping To Neighbour's Roof Will Amount To Mental Cruelty Forming Ground Of Dissolution Of Marriage. Appellant Was Aggrieved By The Impugned Judgment And Decree Passed By The Family Court Dismissing His Application Under Section 13(1)(I—A) Of The Hindu Marriage Act For Grant Of Divorce.

Factual Matrix

Parties Were Married And Their Daughter Was Now Residing With The Respondent/Wife. It Was Submitted That From The Very Next Day Of The Marriage Respondent Insisted To Leave The Matrimonial House, But On Persuasion Stayed For 5-6 Days And Called Her Mother To Return To Her Parental House And Did Not Come Back For 15-20 Days. Later Respondent's Mother Informed The Elderly Persons Of The Society That She Is A Schizophrenic, Which Was Not Informed To The Appellant Before The Marriage.

Incidents Of Abnormal Behaviour

She Used To Call Elderly Persons In The In-Laws' Family By Their Name And On One Night She Jumped To The Neighbour's House From The Roof Of Appellant's House. She Used To Leave Her Matrimonial House Every Now And Then Without Any Rhyme Or Reason. When The Appellant And Other Family Members Objected To Her Behaviour, She Used To Filthily Abuse Them And Locked The Door From Inside. Respondent Denied All The Allegations.

Analysis, Law And Decision

Decisions Pertaining To The Concept Of Mental Cruelty Were Referred To. In The Supreme Court Decision Of Samar Ghosh V. Jaya Ghosh, (2007) 4 SCC 511, Illustrative Cases Where Inference Of Mental Cruelty Could Be Drawn Was Indicated. Supreme Court Decision In V. Bhagat V. D. Bhagat, (1994) 1 SCC 337, Held That Mental Cruelty In Section 13(1)(I—A) Can Broadly Be Defined As That Conduct Which Inflicts Upon The Other Party Such Mental Pain And Suffering As Would Make It Not Possible For That Party To Live With The Other. Mental Cruelty Must Be Of Such A Nature That The Parties Cannot Reasonably Be Expected To Live Together. In Naveen Kohli V Neelu Kohli, (2006) 4 SCC 558, The Supreme Court Held That The Word "Cruelty" Has To Be Understood In The Ordinary Sense Of The Term In Matrimonial Affairs. If The Intention To Harm, Harass Or Hurt Could Be Inferred By The Nature Of The Conduct Or Brutal Act Complained Of, Cruelty Could Be Easily Established. But The Absence Of Intention Should Not Make Any Difference In The Case. In View Of The Above Decisions, Court In The Present Matter Stated That In Light Of The Facts Of The Case, It Can Be Seen That The Respondent-Wife Admitted To Attempting To Commit Suicide And Assaulting Her Mother-In-Law. As Per The Evidence Placed, It Was Stated That The Respondent Once Jumped From The Roof To Fall In The Neighbour's House And Tried To Strangulate Her Daughter And Husband. There Have Also Been Instances Of Respondent-Wife Leaving The House During The Night Hours Wearing White Saree Without Putting Bangles And Vermilion On The Forehead. Hence, Considering The Instance As Stated Above Along With The Psychiatrist Treatment, Bench Held That It Was Sufficient To Prove That Her Conduct Amounted To

Sustained Reprehensible Unjustifiable Conduct Affecting Physical And Mental Health Of The Appellant. When She Attempts To Commit Suicide, This Singular Act By Itself Amounts To Causing Such Mental Cruelty, Which Is Beyond Repair. Bench Noted That In The Present Case There Was Consistent Irresponsible Or Abnormal Behaviour Of The Respondent, Therefore, When The Entire Married Life Is Reviewed As A Whole, Inference Was That The Relationship Was Being Deteriorated And It Was Extremely Difficult For The Appellant-Husband To Live With Respondent-Wife. While Concluding The Decision High Court Expressed That The Wife Was Guilty Of Committing Mental Cruelty, Furnishing A Ground For Dissolution Of Marriage. Trial Court Committed An Error In Not Appreciating The Evidence, Hence The Impugned Judgment And Decree Was Set Aside. [

Rajeshwar Prasad Kaushal V. Gayatri Kaushal

Maintenance Application U/Sec 125 Crpc Cannot Be Decided With Pending Sec 340 Crpc Application: Allahabad High Court

In A Recent Ruling By The Allahabad High Court, It Was Held That A Maintenance Application Under Section 125 Of The Criminal Procedure

Code (Crpc) Cannot Be Decided While There Is A Pending Section 340 Crpc Application, Let Me Provide Some Context And Details About This Case.

The Case Involved A Criminal Revision Filed By The Revisionist, Amit Bajpai, Challenging The Judgment And Order Passed By The Family Court. The Family Court Had Allowed An Application Filed By The Opposite Party No. 2 (The Wife) Under Section 125 Cr.P.C., Directing The Revisionist To Pay Maintenance At The Rate Of Rs. 5,000 Per Month From The Date Of Application (March 17, 2020). However, The Revisionist Had Raised An Important Issue: The Wife Had Allegedly Filed A False Affidavit Claiming To Be A Housewife, While She Was Actually Working As A Physiotherapist At Jai Ram Hospital In Kanpur Nagar.

The Revisionist Had Also Moved An Application Under Section 340 Cr.P.C. On March 31, 2022, Seeking Appropriate Proceedings Against The Wife For Giving A False Affidavit Before The Court. The Family Court Was Aware Of This Pending Application, As Evident From The Order Sheet Dated March 31, 2022. Despite This, The Family Court Proceeded With The Case And Awarded Maintenance To The Wife Based On The Allegedly False Affidavit.

The Allahabad High Court Considered The Issue Of Whether The Decision On The Section 340 Cr.P.C. Application Could Be A Valid Consideration

For Deciding The Section 125 Cr.P.C. Application. The Court Held That Once Findings Are Recorded On The Application Under Section 340 Cr.P.C. And Have Not Been Set Aside By Any Competent Court Of Law, Those Findings Are Binding Upon The Parties. Therefore, The Evidence On Which The Wife Obtained The Judgment In The Proceedings Under Section 125 Cr.P.C. Cannot Be Considered Valid If It Is Based On Evidence That Has Been Held To Be Forged By The Same Court That Decided The Section 125 Proceedings.

In Summary, The Allahabad High Court Emphasized That Pending Section 340 Cr.P.C. Applications Should Be Resolved Before Deciding Maintenance Applications Under Section 125 Cr.P.C. To Ensure Fairness And Accuracy In The Proceedings.

This Ruling Underscore The Importance Of Addressing False Affidavits And Maintaining Integrity In Legal Proceedings.

Neutral Citation No. – 2023:AHC:238266

Case :- CRIMINAL REVISION No. – 3760 Of 2023

Recorded Phone Conversations Admissible As Evidence, Even If Obtained Illegally:

Allahabad High Court

Lucknow Bench Of Allahabad High Court Held That A Recorded Phone Conversation Is An Admissible Piece Of Evidence, And It Cannot Be Discarded Even If Obtained Illegally.

The Bench Held That "The Communication Between The Mobile Phones Of Two Accused Persons When Recorded On A Digital Voice Recorder After Putting The Call On Speaker, Will Not Amount To Interception". A Single-Judge Bench Of Justice Subhash Vidyarthi Passed An Order On A Revision Plea Moved By Mahant Prasad Ram Tripathi, The Former CEO Of Fatehgarh Cantonment Board.

The Petitioner Had Approached The High Court Against The Trial Court's

Order Which Rejected His Discharge Application Seeking Clean Chit In A Bribery Case.

The Petitioner Had Challenged The Proceedings Of The Trial Court On The Ground That The

Entire Case Was Based On The Recording Of A Phone Conversation Which Was Obtained Illegally And Since This Evidence Cannot Be Admissible, The Proceedings Before The Trial Court Were A Futile Exercise.

The Court Rejected The Petitioner's Revision Plea And Held That "Whether The Telephonic Conversation Between The Two Accused Persons Was Intercepted Or Not And Whether It Was Done Legally Or Not, Would Not Affect The Admissibility Of The Recorded Conversation In Evidence Against The Petitioner."

The Bench Highlighted That The Relevance Criteria Is The Only One That Matters In Terms Of Whether Or Not Evidence Is Admissible In India.

Justice Vidyarthi Explained, "The Law Is Clear That An Evidence Cannot Be Refused To Be Admitted By The Court On The Ground That It Had Been Obtained Illegally."

The Petitioner Was Accused Of Demanding Rs 1.65 Lakh In Bribes Through Shashi Mohan, A Member Of The Board. The CBI Had Recorded A Telephonic Conversation Between The Two Accused On A Digital Voice Recorder After One Of The Accused Put The Phone On Speaker. The Co-Accused Allegedly Informed Tripathi During This Exchange That 6% Of The Total Had Been Paid. According To The CBI, Tripathi Answered "Yes" And When Mohan Wanted To Continue The Call, The Former Told Him Not To Bring Up The Subject And Asked Him To Speak With Him In The Office.

Name Of The Case: Mahant Prasad Ram Tripathi @ M.P.R. Tripathi Vs State Of U.P. Via C.B.I./A.C.B., Lucknow And Another

Neutral Citation No. - 2023:AHC-LKO:56067

CRIMINAL REVISION No. - 935 Of 2023

IPC 498-A: Court Cannot Impose Bail Condition On Husband To Resume Marital Life With Wife: Supreme Court

In A Recent Ruling, The Supreme Court Declared That It Is Impermissible To Impose A Condition Requiring An Accused Husband, Seeking Anticipatory Bail Under Section 498A Of The IPC., To Bring His Wife To His Residence And Ensure Her Maintenance And Dignity. The Matter Was Adjudicated By A Division Bench Consisting Of Justices Bela M. Trivedi And Satish Chandra Sharma.

In The Specific Case, The Appellant, Who Was The Accused Husband, Had Filed For Anticipatory Bail With The High Court Of Jharkhand, Ranchi Bench. Although The High Court Granted Bail, It Attached A Unique Condition. This Condition Compelled The Husband To Live With His Wife At His Residence, Taking Responsibility For Her Sustenance While Preserving Her Dignity And Honor. To Provide Clarity, The Condition Is Articulated As Follows:

"Accordingly, The Petitioner Is Directed To Surrender In The Court Within Six Weeks From Today And In The Event Of His Arrest Or Surrendering, He Will Be Enlarged On Bail On Satisfying The Trial Court That The Petitioner Has Taken The Opposite Party No.2 To His House At Bandra Locality Of Ranchi And Keeping And Maintaining Her With Full Dignity And Honour As His Lawful Wife."

Following This Progression, The Husband Appealed To The High Court, Seeking A Reconsideration Of The Mentioned Order. In The Petition Aimed At Modifying The Order, The Husband Contended That He Had Obtained A Residence And Was Willing To Fulfil His Obligations Towards His Wife. In Contrast, The Wife Expressed Her Willingness To Reconcile

And Resume Marital Life, Contingent On Her Husband Joining Her In Their Common Residence. Despite These Arguments, The High Court Dismissed The Husband's Request, Emphasizing That The Appellant Remained Resolute In His Decision Not To Resume Living With His Wife At Their Shared Residence.

"In View Of The Adamant Attitude Of The Appellant In Not Resuming The Conjugal Life With The Opposite Party No.2 In The House Of The Appellant, Where The Opposite Party No.2 Was Staying, His Petition Could Not Be Considered," The High Court Held.

In Light Of This Context, The Matter Was Escalated To The Supreme Court. The Court Emphatically Declared That Imposing Such A Condition Is Not Permissible When Granting Anticipatory Bail. Moreover, This Condition Should Not Be Used As Justification For Rejecting The Appellant's Case.

"In Our Opinion, Neither Such Condition Should Have Been Imposed By The High Court While Granting An Anticipatory Bail, Nor Such Could Be A Ground For Rejection Of The Petition Filed By The Appellant."

In View Of This, While Setting Aside The Impugned Order, The Court Granted Bail To The Accused.

CRIMINAL APPEAL NO.3701 OF 2023

(Arising Out Of SLP (Crl.) No.5695 Of 2023)

Wife's Failure To Comply With Restitution Of Conjugal Rights Decree Ground For Divorce: Karnataka High Court

The Karnataka High Court In The Present Case Took Upon The View That A Failure To Comply With A Decree For Restitution Of Conjugal Rights, Is A Ground For Divorce. The Division Bench Consisting Of Justice S R Krishna Kumar And Justice G Basavaraja, Further Stated That The Refusal Of The Wife To Join The Husband Even After A Decree Of Restitution Of Conjugal Rights Is Sufficient Ground For Divorce Within The Meaning Of Section 13(1A)(Ii) Of The Hindu Marriage Act, 1955.

Facts Of The Case

This Appeal Has Been Filed By The Appellant/Husband Challenging The Decree Passed By The Trial Court, Wherein His Petition Against Respondent/Wife Seeking Divorce On The Ground Of Desertion Was Dismissed By The Trial Court.

The Appellant Was Married To The Respondent And Issued A Legal Notice Calling Upon The Respondent To Join Him, However, The Respondent Refused To Join Him. Upon Which He Instituted A Petition For Restitution Of Conjugal Right. The Said Petition Was Decreed In Favour Of Appellant Ex Parte, As The Respondent Did Not Appear Before The Court. Even After This Decree, The Respondent Did Not Join The Appellant Due To Which He Instituted The Present Petition For Divorce Before The Trial Court. In The Instant Petition Also, The Respondent Remained Ex Parte And Did Not Contest The Petition. Despite This, The Trial Court Refused To Grant Divorce To The Appellant. Aggrieved By This, The Appellant Approached This Court.

Court's Observation And Analysis

The High Court Of Karnataka In The Present Case Made The Observation That The Respondent Had Deserted The Appellant And Was Living Separately From The Year 2013 Onwards. Even After An Ex Parte Decree For Restitution Of Conjugal Rights, The Respondent Did Not Join The Appellant Which Is Sufficient Ground For Divorce Within The Meaning Of Section 13(1A)(Ii) Of The Hindu Marriage Act, 1955. Further, There Has Not Been Any Restitution Of Conjugal Rights Between The Parties For More Than A Period Of One Year After The Decree Was Passed. Further The Division Bench Consisting Of Justice S R Krishna Kumar And Justice G Basavaraja, Held That The Trial Court Committed An Error In Dismissing The Petition Without Appreciating The Above Aspects As Well As The Un-Impeached, Un-Controverted And Unchallenged Pleadings And Evidence Of The Appellant Which Constitute Sufficient Grounds To Grant Decree For Divorce.

Hence, The Karnataka High Court Allowed The Petition Of The Appellant And Dissolved The Marriage Between The Appellant And The Respondent On The Ground Of Desertion By The Respondent.

MISCELLANEOUS FIRST APPEAL NO. 104251 OF 2017 (MC-) Bhimrao Vs Santoshi

Conclusion:

In Navigating The Complexities Of Matrimonial Disputes, The Guidance Provided By The Judiciary Through Supreme Court Judgments And High Court Rulings Serves As A Beacon Of Hope And Empowerment For Husbands Facing False Accusations. As We Conclude This Discussion, It's Imperative To Reflect On The Significance Of Judicial Wisdom In Upholding Justice, Fairness, And Equity In Marital Relationships.

Through Landmark Judgments And Precedent-Setting Rulings, The Judiciary Has Underscored The Importance Of Evidence-Based Decision-Making, Fair Legal Proceedings, And Protection Of Individual Rights. These Principles Form The Bedrock Of Our Legal System, Ensuring That Justice Is Not Only Served But Also Seen To Be Served In Matrimonial Disputes.

As Husbands Seek Solutions And Assistance Amidst The Turmoil Of False Accusations, It's Essential To Harness The Wisdom And Guidance Offered By The Judiciary. By Staying Informed About Legal Precedents, Exercising Their Rights, And Accessing Support Services, Husbands Can Navigate The Legal Landscape With Confidence And Resilience.

Moreover, It's Crucial For Society As A Whole To Recognize The Impact Of False Accusations In Matrimonial Disputes And Work Towards Fostering A Culture Of Fairness, Empathy, And Mutual Respect In Marital Relationships. By Challenging Stereotypes, Promoting Gender Equality, And Advocating For Judicial Reforms, We Can Create A Society Where Justice Prevails, And Families Thrive In Harmony And Peace.

As We Move Forward, Let Us Remain Committed To Upholding The Principles Of Justice, Fairness, And Dignity In Matrimonial Disputes, Guided By The Wisdom And Compassion Of The Judiciary. Together, Let

Us Strive To Build A Future Where Every Individual Is Treated With Respect, Every Voice Is Heard, And Every Dispute Is Resolved With Fairness And Compassion.

Us Strive To Build A Future Where Every Individual Is Treated With Respect, Every Voice Is Heard, And Every Dispute Is Resolved With Fairness And Compassion.